Secrets Of Higher Consciousness

Proven 5-STEP MODEL To Master Your Inner Power and become a CHAMPION!

KUMAR NAGENDRA

STARDOM BOOKS

STARDOM BOOKS

WORLDWIDE

www.StardomBooks.com

STARDOM BOOKS

A Division of Stardom Publishing

and infoYOGIS Technologies.

105-501 Silverside Road

Wilmington, DE 19809

FIRST EDITION AUGUST 2019

Stardom Books

Secrets Of Higher Consciousness/
Proven 5-STEP MODEL To Master Your Inner Power and
become a CHAMPION!

KUMAR NAGENDRA

p. 182
cm. 13.5 X 21.5

Category: Self-help/Mind and Body

ISBN-13: 978-1-7332116-1-1

ISBN-10: 1-7332116-1-6

DEDICATION

I am dedicating this book to "All HUMAN BEINGS"
on this planet EARTH!

CONTENTS

ACKNOWLEDGMENTS

One night, I had a dream, in which someone told me "Kumar why don't you write a book. Your message needs to be put across to millions of people". Till then I had never thought of writing a book. This dream was a trigger point which made me flow towards putting all my life experiences and its learnings I had in the form of a book. Finally, this book is a reality and I am feeling very happy and grateful for all those who were there with me in my journey of writing this book and supported me unconditionally.

Firstly, I am very grateful to the almighty, the God, the Universe for inspiring me to take up this work. Without his guidance this book would not have been possible. Thank You God for your blessings.

I am grateful for the light, which is the source of all creation. This light has always been my guiding force in my life. Thank you Light for being with me always.

I am very grateful to all my gurus and masters who have guided me in this journey. Thank you for your blessings and sharing your valuable knowledge and wisdom which has helped me manifest love, joy, peace and happiness.

I am grateful for my dad Nagendra Rao and grateful for my mom Malathi. They are my backbone for whatever I am today. Have always got their unconditional support and love. I love you Dad, I love you Mom. Thank you so much for everything.

I am very grateful for my wife Amrutha and my son Shikhar. They again are my backbone and my life support. Thank you Amrutha for your unconditional love and support in whatever I do. Thank you Shikhar for being my great source of inspiration. Love you both.

I am very grateful for my "Abundance Team" at Jayanagar, Bangalore. This team is a source of abundant energy which has helped me bring the best out of me. Thank you, Subramanya Sir, Shabana Mam, Kavitha Mam, Sunila Mam, Sunil Roy and Uday.

I would also like to thank all my Quantum leap friends for their continuous support. Your support means a lot to me.

I would like to thank Mr. Surendran J, founder of Success Gyan for bringing the world class trainings to India, which helped me get trained by world's top trainers and leaders.

I would like to thank my international trainers Blair Singer, Robert Riopel, Alex Mandossian, Mac Attram and Vishen Lakhiani for providing me trainings of highest quality which has helped me grow in my life.

I would like to thank my uncle Dr. Y.K. Madhav Rao, who has guided me in writing the chapter on energies.

Special thanks to my dear friend Uday, who has always helped me in my trainings and helped a lot in reviewing this book. Thank you Uday.

I would like to thank my dear friend Syed Umar Ahmed who has helped and supported me always.

I would like to thank my friend Megharaj, who has always supported me.

I have taken few sentences and stories from Internet so that I could articulate my points well. All credit belongs to respective authors.

Last but not the least, I would like to thank my publisher Mr. Ram Anand and his team for helping me publish this book and make this book reach to you.

PREFACE

Why move to your Higher Conscious Levels?

"To be conscious that you are ignorant of the facts is a great step to knowledge."

To solve a problem, first you must know that you have a problem. If you do not know you have a problem how can you solve it. Right?

Many people fall into this category. Where they keep suffering from various problems and feel stuck in different areas of their life and these people do not know what is their actual problem. Once upon a time even I belonged to this category. I had no clue what my problems were.

The root cause why people cannot identify their problems is because they are in their lower conscious levels. When people are in their lower conscious levels, they do not have good awareness about what's happening in and around them. When people live their life with this low awareness and low energy, they live a life of MEDIOCRITY, where life just happens to you.

When people live their life with such mediocrity, they are dishonoring themselves because we humans are born on this planet earth with a great purpose and mission, and when an individual does not live his life with purpose it's a great dishonor to himself. We humans are the most evolved species on this planet and no other species has the powers and potential as that of humans. And that super power we have is "MIND".

Our MIND is so powerful beyond our imagination. Our thoughts and intentions are faster than the speed of light. We need to conquer our MIND, we need to conquer our ENERGIES, so · that we can realize our purpose and mission and live our life with full potential.

Currently most of the people are living a life of a victim, which represents the low level of consciousness. We are born to live a life of EXCELLENCE. We are born to fulfill our MISSION. We are born to live our VISION. We are born to make a DIFFERENCE.

So, why live a life of Mediocrity?

Why do we need to fit in, when we are born to STAND OUT?

To have an amazing life experiences we need to move to our HIGHER CONSCIOUSNESS. When we move to our higher conscious levels we can truly experience love, joy, peace and happiness.

My mission is to help people move to their higher conscious level and through this book I want to fulfill my mission.

Based on my life experiences, my learnings, my research I have put across the solution as to how people can reach their Higher Consciousness in a **5-STEP MODEL** and master their inner power and become a champion in their life. Using this 5-Step model people will have more clarity, more energy and more success.

We need to operate our lives from inside out and not the other way. We need to conquer our Mind and energies and use them to the fullest. Champions are those who conquer their Mind and energies and live their life to the fullest with love, peace, joy and happiness. Champions are those who are strong from within. This 5-step model is all about conquering your Mind and Energies and moving to your Higher conscious levels.

You can see the 5-step model in the next page.

Before we deep dive into these 5 steps, let me take you into my personal journey which is fueled by passion and purpose.

5 - Step Model To Reach Your Higher Consciousness

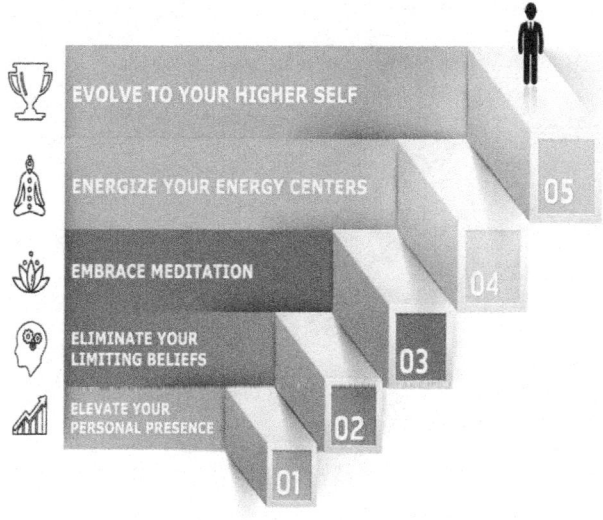

CHAPTER 1:

PERSONAL JOURNEY – FUELED BY PASSION AND PURPOSE

Can you imagine you are having only few minutes to live?

Have you ever been in a situation where time was running out and you had to save someone, or protect?

It was in the year 1992 when I was only six years old, and I had a severe pneumonia attack. It was around 1.30 A.M. in the night when I kept coughing continuously for an hour and was unable to breathe, sit or sleep. My agony knew no bounds and I screamed out in pain when I could no longer take the pain.

Seeing my struggle, my parents started to panic.

Despite giving me all the medicines, injections, my cough and breathlessness were not coming under control. As it was 1.30 A.M., no doctors were available to treat me and not knowing what to do, finally my parents decided to go to our neighbor and seek help.

Our neighbor (both the mother and his son) fortunately were doctors, so it seemed right. My parents rang the doorbell continuously to wake them up. It took some while for our neighbor to open the door and as the door was opened, my parents told them about my condition.

Immediately both the doctors came to my home with their medical kit and examined me. The doctor asked me to open my mouth and probed my tongue. That's it! Immediately he told my father to go to the medical store and get some medicines and injections as quickly as possible. During those days 24/7 medical stores were available only at certain places in Bangalore. So, the doctor gave my father the exact medical store address from where he can get those medicines at that time of the night. The doctor did not tell my parents what exactly had happened to me and he hurried my father to go and get the medication.

In around 30 minutes, my father got the medicines what the doctor had prescribed. Immediately the doctor put on the saline drips to my right hand and gave me about 3-4 different injections into it. I was crying out loud with pain as it was getting more and more difficult for me to breathe. Finally, it took around an hour for the medicine to come into effect. I was able to breathe a little better. Both the doctors were there at my house till 5 A.M in the morning and kept me under observation. That entire night no one slept.

The doctor revealed in the morning that how critical was my situation and told my parents that it was a matter of minutes by which I was saved. Hearing this my parents were in shock and asked the doctor what exactly had happened! To which the doctor replied, "When I first looked at your son's tongue I came to know that he had acute pneumonia and had very little time and hence I asked you to rush and get the medicines." My father asked what had happened to my son's tongue, to which the doctor replied,

"Your son's tongue had turned into **DARK BLUE.**"

Have you ever seen someone's tongue turn into dark blue completely?

By morning around 8:00 A.M. the doctor again examined my tongue and now it had returned to its normal color. The doctor told my parents that there's nothing there to be worried now and that I would be completely fine in a few days. I was treated at my home by this doctor every day for the next ten days. It took me one month to recover, and I could not attend school for that month. My lungs had become weak, and so did my immune system, and I was very vulnerable to infections.

Things were getting better, and I was gaining some strength and started going to school after a gap of one month. As my immune system became so fragile and it was not even more than four months that I had another attack of pneumonia and again I was treated at home for almost one month by the same doctor. It took me another 4 - 5 months to recover completely, and I had to be in utmost care to not to have another pneumonia attack. Due to these severe pneumonia attacks, my lungs had become very weak. I used to have regular asthma attacks, and I utterly relied only on medications.

This suffering continued for another five years, and my entire childhood was spent recovering from asthma attacks whenever it occurred.

When I was around nine years old, my situation came to such an extent that I was addicted to taking steroids prescribed by the doctor, only if I took steroid medicines my asthma would go down, and as soon as I stopped taking steroid medicines my asthma would come back. Due to the side effect of drugs, I had become **BALD** at the center of my head. The baldness at the center of my head was exactly the size of a tennis ball.

Can you imagine a 9-year-old boy becoming BALD?

Got treatment from a dermatologist and got back my lost hair in 3 months. At the age of 10, I was hospitalized thrice in a month due to my severe asthma. It was enough, my parents and I had to find a solution to my health at any cost.

Before telling you, what solution helped me to overcome my health, I want to let you know what were the challenges that I faced during these six years.

I could remember every moment that I suffered for these six years. They say that the most crucial moments of your life are the most happening moments in your life. Whether it is good events or unfortunate, whether it is happiness or pain or the sufferings that you have undergone, you always remember these the most because those events, those memories, those pain, those sufferings will always remain in your subconscious mind and can be easily recollected whenever you want.

You must be wondering.

Why am I telling you all these stories?

What is the connection with this story to move to your higher conscious level?

Every experience that you have will have a connection in the future. You can connect the dots looking behind not looking ahead.

During this journey of 6 years from the age of 6 to 12, I always had a dream to speak on the stage in front of people. I always admired people talking from the stage. I don't know why I had this desire. Every year I used to participate in my school fancy dress competition and enact different characters and speak on the stage for a couple of minutes. This used to make me very happy internally. However, due to my recurring asthma problem, I never took the courage to volunteer myself to speak on stage or never took the initiative to improve and grow my skill of speaking, which I always dreamt of.

The early years of 6 -12 in any child's life play a crucial role as he/she is exposed to various activities to enhance the innate skills such as sports, arts, music, dance etc. But in my childhood journey, it was only about recovering from the recurring asthma attacks. As a child, I never thought of developing a new skill, never thought of learning some new habits and I was never exposed to any of such activities, which a child will typically go through.

Before letting you know how I overcame my asthma problem, let me share with you some of the significant challenges I faced as a child during those six years.

CHALLENGES

1. I had no exposure to the outer world; most of the time I used to be inside the house taking care of my health. My health did not allow me to go outside and play with other children. The moment I used to run I used to get asthma, that's the reason I never played any of the outdoor sports. This is the time when a child explores himself what he likes and what he dislikes, but I had no options. My parents were very supportive, encouraging and loving. They were also very protective of me because of my health reasons. They always did their best as parents. Now today, as I write this book I am also a parent and I realize how important the period from age 6 to 12 is for a child to have a fantastic exposure to different things in their life, laugh, play, enjoy with friends, eat ice-creams, chocolates and be whatever they want to be. I have realized what I have missed in my childhood. I was not allowed to eat ice-creams, chocolates, and fried food because these items would trigger the asthma in me. I was never able to think in terms of what I could have read, what I should learn, but rather my thinking was always about when will my health improve!

Can you imagine going through such tough situations over the period of early years and the mindset that one would have developed?

I had no idea how to think differently, how can you expect me to be creative, be innovative at that age! So, I consider this as one of the significant challenges I faced in my life at that point of time: **NO EXPOSURE TO LIFE.**

2. Another critical factor or the challenge that I had to face because of my health was **Energy Depletion**. What I mean by energy depletion is that, we humans have an

energy system inside us known as Chakras and Auras, which we will be learning in chapter 6. My energy system was affected which reduced my immune system, which made me have repeated attacks again and again because my energy system was depleted and broken. YES! The chakras and Auras were depleted inside me because of which I was very vulnerable to other outside factors that could affect me and bring my energy down and not get me motivated anymore.

Neither myself nor my parents had any knowledge about these energies at that point of time, and we never thought about this factor called energies which would affect us. One major thing which everyone should be aware of is how these energies play an essential role inside and outside of us in our wellbeing, in our health, in our success and whatever we do.

During all these years of struggle, I never had any energy left in me to do something useful. I always used to have very less energy and used to get tired very quickly, and because of this, I could not do anything I wanted to do. This is also one of the reasons why I did not have the mindset to learn new things and did not enhance my speaking skills, which I always dreamt off.

So, to put it in one sentence: Energy Depletion, no exposure to the outside world, always being inside the home and no any sports activities were some of my significant challenges during the age of 6 to 12.

It was high time that I had to overcome these challenges at any cost. We had to try something new. One day my parents thought why don't we put our son to yoga. Resistance and the immune system must be developed at any cost only then this problem will be solved permanently. They took me to one place in Chamrajpet in Bangalore to a lady by the name Dr. Nagarathna. She is one of the pioneers in the field of Yoga therapy. After listening to my case, she understood there is only one remedy, and I need to go and learn yoga in a residential camp for one month where they would be teaching and training yoga for my specific problem. We immediately agreed for this and decided that my mother would accompany me and stay along with me for one month in the residential yoga camp. This residential yoga was taught at a place called Swami Vivekananda yoga Kendra - Prashanti Kutiram, Jigani near bannerghatta. This place is located a few kilometers outside of Bangalore.

Going to this residential yoga was one of the turning points in my life as this was a tremendous help to my health. I got trained on different yoga Asanas that would help me overcome my asthma. During this training of one month, I had a fantastic experience of my life. I made terrific friends of different ages. I had to follow a completely different routine according to their rules, which was a little difficult in the beginning but then got used to those routines. I had to follow a strict diet based on the food given by the camp. This place was entirely away from the city and was surrounded by trees, and it was like living in the middle of the forest, which made me feel very calm and refreshed.

After completing one month of residential yoga camp, I was given a plan on how to follow yoga and diet at home. I practiced religiously the routine that they had planned for me for the next three months. As time progressed I started to develop my immune system and gradually my asthma attacks frequency reduced. After around two years of doing yoga consistently, I gained my strength, my confidence and most important got back my health.

Yoga was a life changer for me; if not for yoga I don't know what my health would have been by now. I am grateful for those people who taught me yoga and very thankful to my parents for introducing yoga into my life.

Some of the life learnings I learned or realized after many years for this period of my life (Age 6 -12) when I reflected my childhood journey.

- Health is the most crucial aspect of one's life; without health you are nothing.
- For every problem there is a solution; we need to persist in finding the right answer. There will be many alternative paths to seek the solution.

- Due to specific incidences in our life, certain beliefs would be set inside us. We need to see whether those beliefs are limiting beliefs or not which are stopping us from moving ahead (We will explore Beliefs part in upcoming chapters). This learning about beliefs was such a significant game changer in my life.
- Children should be taught to focus more on health and fitness from a very young age say from the age of 4 - 5 itself. Here parenting plays a vital role.
- Children should be exposed to many good things in life at a very early age.

Life was reasonable, and my health improved significantly as time progressed. Talking about my studies, I always thought that I am an average student even though I was good at it. See, how one's perception of themselves plays a crucial role.

As I had mentioned earlier that I always had this desire and admiration for people speaking on stage, somewhere inside my heart I always wanted an opportunity to talk on stage in front of people. I don't know why I had his strong desire to speak in front of people, but somehow, I wanted to be on stage and feel very good about it. I want to say that this dream was deeply rooted in my subconscious mind.

Most people during their late adolescent age (17-19 years) would not be clear on their purpose of life. I was also one among the majority group who had no idea about my life's purpose. Probably, I never had a single thought about things such as "Purpose, Mission and Vision." As I said earlier, I had very little exposure to the world and did not know what all options we had to choose for our careers and that we could choose any based on our choice/interest.

After completing my board exams (10th), my classmates and I were saying goodbye to our teachers. At that point, one of my teachers asked me "Kumar, how about going to IIT (Indian Institute of Technology) after your 12th, have you started preparing from now itself or have you enrolled to any tuitions to

prepare? It's better you start preparing yourself from now itself."
For which I said, "No mam, I have not started preparing, I will
think about it." She said, "How come you have not thought about
it? Many students start preparing from 9th std itself." By this time,
I was feeling uncomfortable talking to my teacher because just now
I had finished my 10th board exams, for which I had been studying
day and night for few months and here comes my teacher telling
me to consider for some nonsense IIT course from 9th std itself
and talking about attending tuitions.

Honestly speaking, I had no idea what IIT was and the value of
it. I heard the word "IIT" for the first time. Indian Institute of
Technology colleges are the most famous institutes in India for
studying Engineering. These are the prestigious institutes to study
from India. It took me another one month to know about IIT's
and how to study for those entrance examinations and the value of
studying in those institutes. Such was my level of exposure and
knowledge.

When I was in my 12th standard, I somehow got an
opportunity to speak on stage for 5 minutes. It was one of the
college's annual dance function. I was given a chance to talk on
stage about the event and about the dance themes that was going
to take place. The stage was set, around 200 people were in the
auditorium, I was ready with my script to speak on stage, all the
dancers were waiting in their costumes, a music system and the
lighting was set, and the show was about to begin. I was waiting
for this moment since my childhood. I was very much excited that
I will be speaking in front of a huge crowd. I had byhearted my
script thoroughly. The stage was big, and there was a standing mic,
which was placed in the middle of the scene.

Finally, my turn had come to go on stage and speak and feel
good about this opportunity.

I was not nervous but was very excited and thrilled to be on
stage. I went on stage in front of the mic and saw around 200
people looking at me. I had never stood before in front of such a
big crowd. All the lights were focused entirely on me. I did not take
my script with me on the stage because I was confident in

remembering my script. I went on the stage, and I could hear people still speaking here and there in the crowd.

I began my speech well and continued for 20 seconds.

Suddenly I went completely BLANK, and no words flowed through my mind. I was clueless about what was happening to me at that moment. I completely forgot my speech and stood there in the middle of the stage in silence. Not a single thought was flowing into me.

I was dead frozen like a Cat.

My reptilian brain was hijacked and was threatened at that moment.

I stood there like a fool in the middle of 200 people not speaking anything for almost 30 seconds. My friend, who was hosting the show was calling me from the side of the stage "Kumar speak, speak, what happened to you?" After around freezing for 30 seconds on stage, suddenly I realized I have been standing here in front of the crowd not speaking anything for quite some time,

I said "**SHIT**" in front of the mic keeping my right hand on my head. People heard what I uttered and some of them probably in the front two rows started laughing at me.

I had not realized that I had uttered the word "SHIT". When I heard some people laughing in the audience only then, I again realized that I had uttered this nonsense word in front of the mic, for this realization I again uttered this nonsense word "SHIT" in front of the mic by mistake. All my senses were back, and my blood started gushing all through my body at a rapid pace and I started feeling the heat and my hands and legs started shaking tremendously. My lips were dry, and my voice was choked, and I could not tolerate this humiliation anymore. Though all my senses were back, I wanted to run away from the stage, but my legs were still frozen and was unable to move an inch from the stage. Somehow, I gathered courage and with great difficulty, said "SORRY" and ran away from the stage and from college and did not attend college for the next three days.

Can you imagine yourself being in that situation?

This was the most embarrassing moment in my life so far...I would say more than embarrassing it was the most horrifying incident of my life!

For the next two days, my heart was still beating at a very high rate, I could feel my blood still hot inside, and tremendous FEAR was set inside me. I did not speak with anyone for two days. My friend who witnessed this incident could not contact me as he did not know where my home was located and during those days I did not have a mobile phone.

This one incident had turned my life completely upside down. This incident had a profound impact on my life. I suffered this humiliation for eight years in my life.

I lost my self-esteem, self-confidence, and courage to speak naturally with others. Fear was set inside me that what if it happens again to me when I am talking with others! I had lost all hope and I thought that I will never be able to speak again on stage confidently. I never told this to my parents nor to my close friends, who could have probably helped me. I kept all these things to myself and suffered the pain for eight long years.

Can you relate to this when some similar incidents in your life have set the fear inside you to move ahead?

Significant Challenges I faced due to this incident.

- **I was CONFINED to myself for eight long years:**

After that incident, my life completely changed for the worst. All my dreams and desires were shattered. I had no courage to tell anyone about this incident. I tried telling my parents about this incident many times but could not. I simply could not gather courage to bring it up. A layer of fear was set inside me, and this layer grew thicker day by day and became a big wall of doubt in my life.

I lost my natural ability to speak comfortably with people. I interacted only with few people for these eight years. This negative impact was deeply rooted in my subconscious mind. I wanted to ask for help to overcome this suffering, but I had no courage to ask for help. My mindset was utterly changed from positive to negative, and all wrong limiting beliefs were set inside me. I always stayed within myself in whatever I did. I used to be a silent spectator wherever I went to, be it in college, in my studies, with friends or in any functions. As days and months passed by I had created a small circle of the comfort zone of being confined to myself. I stayed in this small circle of the comfort zone for eight long years.

Can you relate to this?

Have you ever been in such situations in your life?

- **Had very Low Self-Esteem and low Self-Confidence:**

Due to this incident, my self-esteem was crushed; my self-esteem went to such a low level you can never imagine. Due to this low self-esteem, my self-confidence also shattered. I stopped doing YOGA. I did not give importance to myself. I blamed myself too often. I was not able to put forth my opinions whenever I had conversations. I started wasting time by watching all the movies that came on television. My butt was glued to the sofa because I had no confidence in doing something new afresh.

Can you imagine what happens when your self-esteem and self-confidence is crushed down to earth?

- **Lived a MEDIOCRE LIFE:**

First and foremost, I stopped dreaming.
Never took up any new challenges in life.
I had no goals in life.
I had no proper daily routine.
I had no clarity in what I was doing.
I was not able to enjoy whatever I did.

I felt restless and lonely.

I had no personal development and growth.

I had no Inspiration and internal motivation to do something.

I did not have a single thought or intention to contribute or add value to people's life.

I just lived a mediocre life!

Have you anytime experienced such things in your life?

- **Fear of Speaking again on Stage:**

This was my ultimate challenge for the next eight years after the incident. Immense fear had set inside me from speaking on stage again. I had no hope that I will ever talk again on stage. I tried my level best to come out of this fear but was not successful. I felt all the doors were closed for me. Front, back, left, right, top and bottom, there was no way to escape. I continued to suffer all alone not giving a clue to anyone about my internal feelings and situations. A dream, a desire of speaking on stage again looked very far from reality. Big Rocky Mountains had appeared between myself and my goals.

Have you ever witnessed such mountains between you and your dreams?

LIGHT at the end of TUNNEL

Most of them say, that there is always light at the end of the tunnel. I kept hearing this again and again during this journey of 8 years. I had faith that I will be able to come out of this situation. Finally, one day light did appear at the end of my tunnel.

A ray of hope appeared through my mentor.

He showed me the below diagram which changed my life for good. Even though I had come across those five words very often individually, it did not create any change in me until I saw those five words together in this diagram.

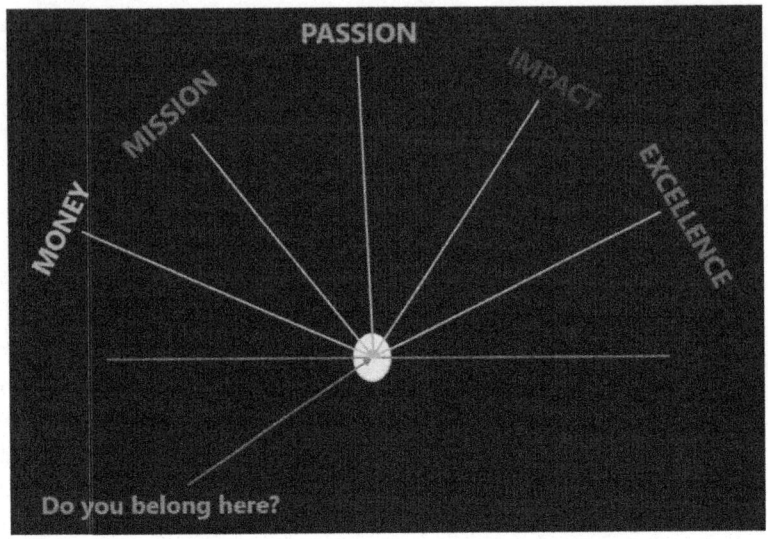

PASSION, IMPACT, EXCELLENCE, MISSION, and **MONEY** were the most potent words at that moment which together radiated some unknown high energy into me which suddenly removed the significant layer of clutter from my mind. I was waiting for this trigger for eight years to happen. In a moment, I just asked this one question to myself: "Do I belong to the intersection of these five lines?" The answer was "Absolute BIG NO." I scored a BIG "ZERO" in all these five parameters in my life.

How about you?

PASSION

'Are you insanely passionate about something in your life?" was the question I asked myself. I had no idea about what I was passionate about in my life. Just lived a mediocre life.

Are you able to transmit your passion and positive energy to others? Passion is something that you have strong feelings and emotions about doing a thing. It could be your work that you do, or any activities like singing, dancing, any sports, public speaking, acting, cooking, writing, teaching, training, etc., which gives you a sense of satisfaction, happiness, and joy.

IMPACT

"Are you inspiring and creating a positive impact on people's lives, careers, business in a BIG way? Are you creating value for the people or the world?" These were the questions I asked myself. I was nowhere near creating IMPACT in other people's lives. Forget about other people, I had not produced any positive impact on my life itself.

EXCELLENCE

"Are you the best in your domain? Are you an expert and belong to the top one percent in the world in your topic of the domain?" Again, these were the questions I asked myself. I guess, I need not tell you. You know the answer very well. Yes, again the answer to this question was "BIG NO."

MISSION in your Life

"Do you have a mission in your life? Do you know the purpose of your life? Why are you here on this planet earth? What's the one big mission that you are born to accomplish?" These were the questions that started ringing loudly in my mind, and I had no answers.

MONEY

"Do you make satisfactory money?" My answer was "BIG NO," and this would be the answer to most of us. Money is a significant factor in our lives. No one can deny it.

I firmly believe that **"You can give only what you have."**

When you don't have something, how can you give something back to others? Let it be anything. If you don't have love within you, how can you give love to others? If you don't have knowledge and wisdom within you, how can you provide that knowledge and wisdom to others? If you want to help or contribute to a large community monetarily and you don't have money, how can you help monetarily? So first you need to make money satisfactorily.

Imagine what the world will be if the answer to all the above questions could be a **huge YES?**

I wanted such a life for myself - at the intersection of all the five lines inside that circle.

I wanted to live my life profoundly and intensely. I wanted to live my life with passion, create an huge impact on people's lives, wanted to be the best in what I do, wanted to live and fulfill my mission and make satisfactory money in my life.

That night I did not sleep; all these questions were running in my mind. I had to find answers to all these questions and take massive actions to change my life. After deep thought, that night, that moment I decided enough is enough at any cost I am coming out of this situation and creating a life for myself where I belong to the intersection of those five lines. There was a spark of light inside me. For the next two weeks, I was searching answers to all the above questions.

Again, my mentor Sandeep Gupta helped me discover the answers

As I have mentioned earlier that I always liked and got inspired from people speaking on stage. I still had that desire inside me to speak in front of people and impact their lives positively.

"I committed to myself that I will be a world class Professional Speaker and a Trainer."

So, that's how

"I found my passion for SPEAKING and TRAINING."

Below is the list of things I did to improve myself:

-    I trained and worked hard on my personal growth, worked on my self-esteem, self-confidence every single day.

Even today I work on improving my personal growth because I believe that this is one of the most critical aspects one should keep developing to achieve their ultimate purpose.

- Enhanced my speaking and training skills by attending seminars and workshops.

- Read lots of books on personal development.

- Started researching on mind powers relentlessly and began implementing them. Such as Thoughts, Intentions, Visualizations, memory techniques, etc...

- Initially, I got trained and certified to be a Trainer by Asia's No. 1 success coach Dr. Bharath Chandra.

- Joined Garden City Toastmasters club in Bangalore and improved my speaking skills. I must thank my office colleague **Rajatha**, who introduced me to this Garden City Toastmasters club.

- I did my Speechcraft certification at this Toastmasters club.

- Started meeting new amazing people and created a big circle of friends from various industries.
- Started studying the powers of mind and begun implementing in my life and saw significant benefits in my personal life.

- Started developing different perspectives of the world and life. I would say having different perspectives of life will do wonders in your life. Having different perspectives helped me a lot. How about you? Do you try to see things differently or see things the same way as most of the people do? I suggest you try giving a thought about having different perspectives and see the difference.

- Attended many workshops, seminars, boot camps, various talks over the years and this is my ongoing habit to learn and grow consistently. I can't say how much value it adds to your life.

- Slowly came over my public speaking fear by giving small talks at my Toastmaster's club and also at various places whenever I got opportunities.

Through one of my friend Kiran, I got an opportunity to be a part of the Knowledge Sharing Platform (KSP). A forum started for all trainers and speakers to share their knowledge and wisdom to people. We conducted four projects / seminars in Bangalore within a year.

I delivered talks on the below three topics in three seminars.

- POWER OF NOW
- YOU-PASSION
- LAW OF ATTRACTION

Among all the speakers/trainers, I was the youngest speaker in all the seminars that we conducted. The audience appreciated all my talks and told me you have a high potential to speak on stage; you are energetic, enthusiastic, you speak from your heart, etc. I started to feel and sense that **"Yes I have started to live my PASSION."** This instilled so much of happiness and peace within me.

I continued my research on mind powers, was reading a lot of books, articles and was watching videos about the mind and its hidden powers. Tried experimenting with the techniques learned, some of the methods gave impressive results, and some did not. I slowly progressed in my life and was a much confident person now.

A Twist:

Even though I was now a confident person, used many techniques of Mind Powers and saw good results, all was not flowing smoothly in my life. I was STUCK in many areas of my life: Financial stability, Health, Career, and Spirituality. I was not growing enough especially in these significant areas of my life. Things were not free-flowing in these areas, there were many blocks and obstacles which I was not able to see and identify.

Have you ever felt stuck in life (where things are not flowing freely) even though you thought you had great will power, self-confidence, and a healthy mindset?

Same was my case. This lead me to find a solution to this problem. After researching many different aspects of life, reading many books, speaking to lots of people, observing the environment around me, one thing was for sure which I had missed paying attention to.

It was "ENERGIES."

It was the lack of awareness on energies inside us and around us. Energies play a massive role in our lives. Everything in this universe has its own Energy. As I started studying more in-depth into this subject, I learned some of the fantastic things about Human energy system which is about Chakras (The seven main energy centers in Humans) and Auras (Human Energy field around us). Learned about Energy blocks and how they affect us in daily life — learned how to energize our chakras and Auras and remove those energy blocks in us and live a life of abundance.

Took up Meditation seriously as part of my life and saw tremendous improvement in all areas of my life especially in Financial and Spiritual growth. I was able to grow more than 150% financially in less than a year. Before this, for four years I was financially stagnant. When I say, I was able to grow spiritually. What I mean by Spiritual is that I was able to know more about myself, my inner self, my real purpose, I was ready to go deep within myself. Many opportunities started coming my way, my quest to learn and grow increased every day.

I got trained and Internationally certified by one of the world's best coaches T. Harv Eker and Blair Singer to be a professional trainer and enhanced my skills of speaking and training through various intense pieces of training for over a period of 2 years. Using Mind power techniques and unlocking my energies I elevated my CONSCIOUSNESS. Also, I finally found my Life's MISSION and VISION.

My Life's Mission:

*"INSPIRE, TEACH AND TRAIN HUMAN BEINGS
TO REACH THEIR HIGHER CONSCIOUS LEVELS SO
THAT THEY LIVE THEIR LIFE WITH PASSION, JOY,
HAPPINESS AND LOVE."*

My Vision:

*"To reach out to a Million (10 Lakhs) people in next five
years and train them to reach their higher conscious levels."*

I have started my journey to live my vision with passion and fulfill my Mission and make a difference in people's life.

The journey of Human life is a gift given to this human race on this planet earth by the ultimate power in the universe. It is up to you and me to make this journey a beautiful one and have wonderful experiences on this planet earth. For this to happen, you should move into your higher conscious levels, where the experiences you have will bring you true happiness, joy, and peace.

Now we will deep dive into 5 step Model to move into your Higher Conscious levels and live your life with great energy, great experiences and have More Clarity. More Energy. More Success.

Are you excited and ready to deep dive step by step to reach your Higher Consciousness?

5 - Step Model To Reach Your Higher Consciousness

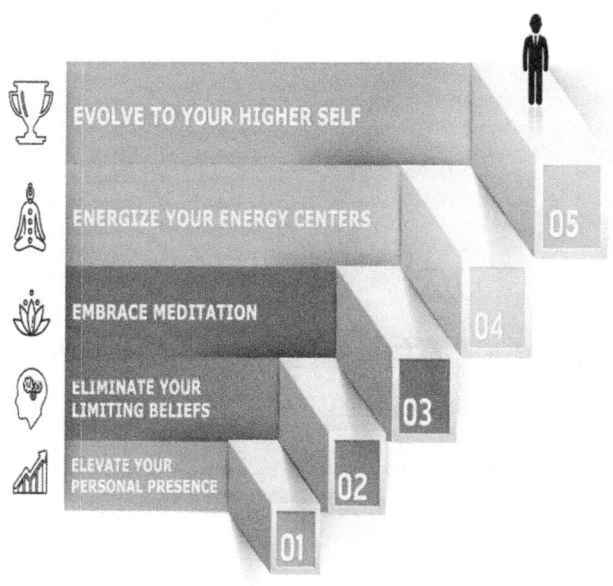

Step 1 - ELEVATE your Personal Presence

5 - Step Model To Reach Your Higher Consciousness

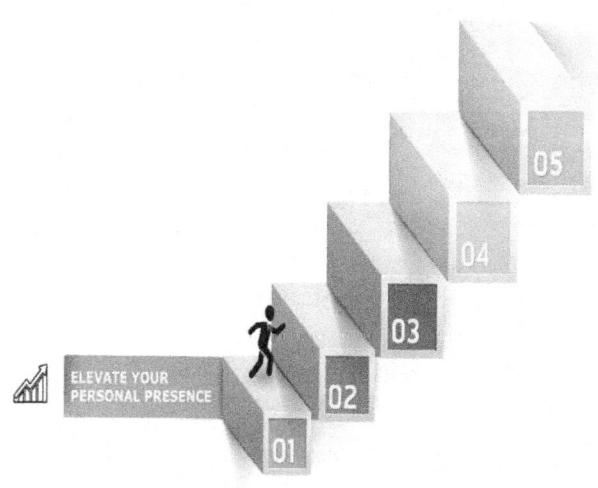

KUMAR NAGENDRA

CHAPTER 2:

THE POWER OF PERSONAL PRESENCE

"Life is available only in the Present moment"
- Thich Nhat Hanh

The most beautiful thing in life is the experiences you have every second and being aware of it. But are we aware of these experiences? I would say to some extent we are aware, but while acquiring most of the lessons we are not. Most of us considerably pay less attention on purpose, and very few of us pay attention to detail consciously.

Do you belong to the group where you pay attention to your day to day experiences on purpose most of the time? If so, then you are on the journey to move into your higher conscious levels.

If you don't belong to this group, there's nothing to worry! You can always start paying attention to your daily experiences from today. Start paying attention right now and begin your journey to move into your higher consciousness. Personal presence is the most basic and fundamental thing you must have at the root level in your life.

By practicing personal presence, you can have tremendous benefits in your life. But so far most of the people have given very less importance to personal presence, and due to this, they are having many problems in their life.

What is Personal Presence?

Personal presence is being aware of all your six senses. Each of the five physical senses gives you a different perspective of the experience. Consider an example of how you could experience heavy rain occurring in the forest through your senses (Seeing the lush green forest and rain, hearing rain and birds in the woods, smelling the freshness of pure air and surrounding atmosphere, feeling the raindrops soaking in your skin and eating the delicious hot food in the cold weather). These five physical senses work all the time whether you are aware of it or not.

How much awareness do you have about your senses?

The sixth sense that we need to be aware of is called INTUITION. Each one of us has this power of intuition, but we use it very rarely to its full capacity.

Let me tell you:

"In the next 2 decades, Intuition will be the core learning for many individuals, corporates and schools. Because through intuition we can access huge sources of knowledge, which otherwise is difficult to attain through traditional learning. Accessing your intuition brings in more clarity in your life, which is the key to your journey of life."

Personal presence is all about awareness in which we live. Liveliness is awareness. Since people do not practice being in their own presence, people's consciousness is limited, and it is in its low vibration. It is every individual's responsibility to increase their awareness of higher vibrations.

"Your awareness is not strong enough. It is not lighting up the whole space. You are lighting up only one corner of your life. This awareness only allows you to survive in this world. This awareness is not enough to know the nature of life. If you need to know the nature of your existence, you need to elevate your awareness to a higher level." – Sadhguru

Personal presence is about being in both **Body and Mind**. Being in Personal presence is more about the Self. We can categorize Personal presence into 2 types:

1. Inner Presence
2. Outer Presence

We will discuss these 2 types of presence in detail a bit later. Let's first consider the benefits of being in Personal presence.

Benefits of being in Personal Presence

The benefits of being in personal presence is limitless. If you practice the techniques of being in your own presence consciously and consistently, then I am sure you can take your life to its next higher level.

Some of the remarkable benefits you will have being in your Personal Presence are:

- You will be *less STRESSFUL*
- You will be *less ANXIOUS*
- You will be *less FEARFUL*
- You will be *more PRODUCTIVE*
- You will have *more CLARITY*
- You will be *more HAPPIER*

And the most important is. You will be **LESS WORRIED**. As you know Worrying is the primary cause for most of the illness. We worry unnecessarily about the future which we do not know and fear about the past which we cannot change. We add lots of stress to our body by worrying, which causes the body's sympathetic nervous system to release stress hormones such as Cortisol. These stress hormones can cause reactions such as-

1. Difficulty to swallow
2. Dizziness
3. Increase in Heartbeat
4. Headaches
5. Fatigue
6. Not able to focus and concentrate
7. Irritability
8. Muscle Aches
9. Shortness of breath
10. Sweating
11. Suppression of the immune system
12. Digestive disorders
13. Heart Attacks
14. Depression and suicidal thoughts

The list goes on. **Research shows that almost 70 percent of the diseases and illness are caused due to worrying, stress, and anxiety.** This is proved by top researchers. These 3 elements of the human disorder are interlinked, and these can be eliminated by Elevating your **Personal Presence.** Personal presence plays a vital role in one's life. The more you practice personal presence the greater the benefits you see in your life.

As we saw what could be the benefits of being in personal presence, it's also important to know why most of the people are not in their own presence.

Reasons why people are not in Personal Presence

The biggest reason why people are not in personal presence is **ANXIETY.** People are mainly anxious about something terrible is going to happen to them such as a significant failure, health problems, accident, death, rejection, etc. This anxiety is due to unknown fear set inside most of us due to various negative external factors. When people are anxious and worried how can they be in their personal presence.

The second primary reason for people not being in personal presence is *Physical Body Tiredness*. The tired physical body contributes to not being in personal presence. It has its own mechanism cycle. When the body gets tired, you cannot be in the present. It's important to identify the moment when your body starts to get tired and give it a break or rest for some time. But most of us do not recognize this awareness of tiredness of our body and we tend to continue working making the body more exhausted and only give rest until your body cannot take any longer. This is one of the common mistakes most of us make.

So, what is lacking is adequate **REST** for your body. So, I guess you know what to do.

Another reason for people not being in personal presence is **EGO**. Yes, Ego does not allow you to be in your own presence. Having a high ego does not allow you to connect to this beautiful world around you. Being in personal presence will enable you to identify your ego and helps you to reduce your ego consciously and effortlessly.

And the *latest addition* to the reasons for people not being in personal presence is **TECHNOLOGY**. Yes, no doubt technology has helped humans to live a more comfortable life, but people are getting more addicted to technology. People are hooked on to their devices rather than to connect with people surrounding them. So many distractions such as social media, notifications of apps, text messages, emails, etc. Wherever you see at home, offices, airport lounge, canteens, streets, etc. you find people glued onto devices rather than conversations with people.

Being in your personal presence consciously helps you to balance out between technology and people around you to connect directly with less material things and more human beings.

These were some of the primary reasons I wanted to bring in front of you. Before practicing personal presence, it was essential to identify the reasons why people are not in their own presence any more. This helps you to learn and practice personal presence better.

A Beautiful exercise to do:

"Your personal presence grows to the extent you do."

During my early days of using personal presence, I came across this beautiful exercise, which gave me a sense of meaning and a different perspective of life.

Say suppose there is a machine that gets invented which can be plugged into your brain and removes all your past memories from your mind. What will happen? Will you have any problems from the past or any worries? No right?

Steps:

1. Close your eyes and imagine as if you have set up a fire in front of you, and you are going to drop one of your most precious things into it. What is that valuable thing that you are going to sacrifice?
2. YOUR MEMORY
3. Now bundle up all your memory from the beginning of your life and put it into that fire.
4. Now open your eyes and identify who you are? All your thoughts have gone, all your past memories have gone. You are just like a NEWBORN BABY.
5. Whoever you are, you are a beautiful person. Is this person good or bad? You do not know.
6. Just look at everyone (or imagine people whom you know) around you and do you find anything wrong in anyone?

When you don't remember anything from the past, you are just being in the present moment and flowing through it. At this moment when you see other people, you see them as another beautiful person, and you are in joy just like a small baby.

Do the above exercise for at least 2-3 mins before reading further and try to feel what you feel by imagining the above.

When and where should you be in Personal Presence

"Presence should always be <u>INSIDE OUT</u>."

Presence should be first in the **MIND**, then in the **Body** and then into your **Surroundings**. If you miss this order, you misfire your true powerful personal presence. I believe you should be in your own presence "Always," if not you need to be at least "most of the time" in your personal presence to achieve higher consciousness and grow in all areas of your life.

As I had mentioned earlier, we have 2 types of personal presence. The inner presence and outer presence. Let's learn in depth about these 2 types of presence with the help of UNIVERSAL PRESENCE MODEL.

UNIVERSAL PRESENCE MODEL

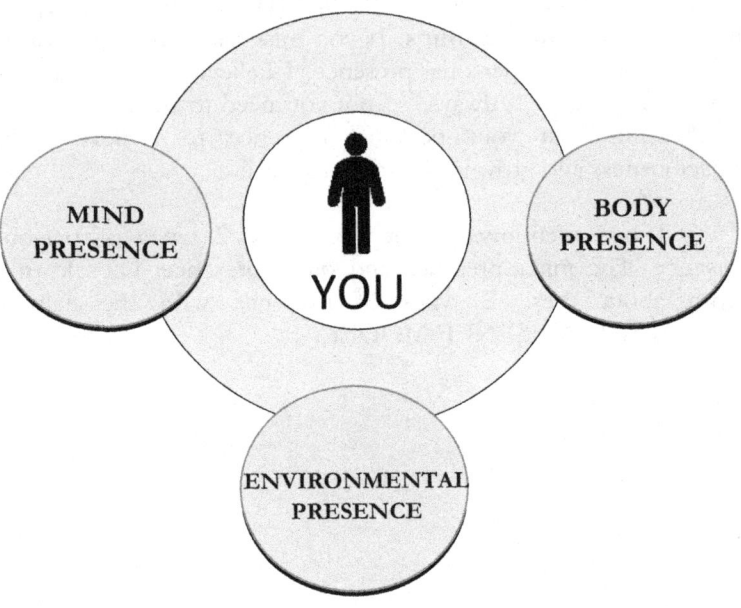

Universal presence model consists of 3 components:
1. MIND PRESENCE (Inner presence)
2. BODY PRESENCE (Inner and Outer presence)
3. ENVIRONMENTAL PRESENCE (Outer presence)

MIND PRESENCE

"It's all about being aware of your THOUGHTS, INTENTIONS, and EMOTIONS."

THOUGHTS

The thought is nothing but what we "Think". Every second of our life when we are awake we think, i.e., we generate thoughts continuously.

What is the quality of your thoughts?

Are you aware of your thoughts?

If "Yes," how much are you aware of your thoughts? If "No," why are you not aware of your thoughts?

Thoughts are very much responsible for everything that happens in your life. Your thoughts influence your behavior and control your actions.

Awareness of your thoughts is very critical for your wellbeing. How often do you consciously become aware of your thoughts and their quality? Whether you have good thoughts or bad thoughts?

When I say good thoughts, they are nothing but high vibrational thoughts which can elevate you and when I say bad thoughts they are low vibrational thought which can put you down with low energy and make you feel stressed.

INTENTIONS

"Intention is the starting point of all your manifestation."

Intention is a superpower that fulfills all your needs (whether it is money, relationships, love, spiritual, etc.) in every area of your life.

Are you consciously aware of all the intentions with which you are moving forward?

Are you aware of the quality of your intentions?

Everything happens twice. First in mind with intention and only then in this physical reality. Most of the time we do our daily activities without being aware of our intentions consciously.

When we carry out specific actions daily without knowing the intentions behind, we are performing this action subconsciously, and most of the time this action does not have the clarity in what you are doing. So, it is essential to be aware of your intentions and its quality.

EMOTIONS

"If you are not being aware of your Emotions, you cannot control or change them."

What kind of emotion or feeling are you in most of your day? Do you feel good, calm, happy and energetic? Or Do you feel sad, angry, upset, depressed and tired? Are you consciously aware of your Emotions?

Are you able to have a balanced state of emotion throughout the day?

Does your emotional stability fluctuate every now and then to extremes in a day or two?

Are you aware of your emotions? If you are not aware of your feelings, you can get carried away with that emotion. Some of the emotions can be destructive and can impact on your behavior.

Being aware of your emotions helps you achieve better health, better relationships and enables you to become a better leader and a better person.

So, to practice Mind presence in your daily life below is the simple exercise that you can implement.

Mind Presence Exercise:

"Every 1 hour, pause for 1 minute and look back at your Thoughts, Intentions and Emotions that you had and check their quality".

Check what kind of thoughts were running in your mind, whether they were high quality positive thoughts or low quality thoughts or were they average thoughts. Also check whether you had too many thoughts running down your mind which made you feel stressed / Overwhelmed / tensed or you had less thoughts which were clam and peaceful.

Similarly, check whether you had set any positive intentions in that period and if so whether you were able to focus on that intention or not. Check in what emotion you were operating in that period. Whether your emotion was same or fluctuating.

By doing this exercise repetitively, what you are doing is, you are conditioning your Mind to follow a pattern. This repetitive Mind presence exercise will help you have and develop high vibrational thoughts, intentions and emotions consciously.

BODY PRESENCE

"Being aware of your physical body (both inside and outside) and its expressions."

Body presence is more to do with physical appearance, body language, expressions and communication with others.

You need to be aware and feel the pain, stiffness, and stretch, of your muscles while doing exercises. Are you being aware what's happening inside your body consciously?

You also need to be aware and feel the relaxation in your body when you relax. Relaxation is the bridge between your Mind and Body.

Your body language tells a lot about yourself and your behavior and communication. Are you being aware of whether your body language and your thoughts and intentions are in sync or not?

Body presence is more of an outer presence than inner presence. Do you feel every part of your physical body consciously? Do you involve every part of your body when in action? Do you observe the sensations and tingling in your body when you have different life experiences? Do you feel and observe tiredness and stress in your physical body?

Only when you are aware of sensations happenings in your body, you can take appropriate actions. The most significant advantage of being present in your body is that you can impact and inspire many people in your life because you are more grounded, and this helps you take better and massive actions in your life.

One of the best life lessons that I learned is that by being more aware of my body and its sensations, I was able to take significant actions in my life, which has helped me progress faster in my life and helped me be a better human being. And one of the best ways to practice body presence is:

"Practice physically the way you want to speak, act or perform before the actual event/performance takes place."

Don't try to be perfect. Be in your natural flow. Your presence is built over time. When you create this presence and maintain it consistently, people feel your presence with impact and impression.

Always have a confident posture physically. This will resonate along with your inner self: Mind presence.

Body Presence Exercise:

"Every 55 mins pause for 30 seconds and stretch your muscles and feel every part of your body".

ENVIRONMENTAL PRESENCE

"Being aware of your environment, of what is around you, surrounding you."

Your environment is surrounded by nature such as trees, rivers, mountains, wind, animals, birds, rain, etc. You are also surrounded by many beautiful people. For most of us, it's people of different kinds- be it at home, workplace, events, parties or any other place you choose to go.

Your environment also consists of many inanimate objects or non-living things such as buildings, vehicles, devices, furniture and many other things to name.

The most important and only thing for you to be in environmental presence is **"To Connect"** to your environment.

Connect with nature, connect with the people around you, connect with the animals, plants. Create trust in you.

Now you may ask me how can we get connected to buildings, vehicles and other non-living things in this world? There is a way to do that through Energies and vibrations, which we will see in Step 4: Energize your Energy centers. Everything in this universe is Energy which is vibrating at different frequencies.

The best way to connect effectively with other people is not by speaking, but by **listening**.

Another best way to connect with anyone is a *"SMILE."* A smile is a powerful tool, which helps to build your presence physically, mentally and environmentally.

Can you now *SMILE* at people in your room or a place where you are reading this book now and see how you get connected and know how you feel?

Another way to connect is by saying **"Thank You"** with a big smile on your face. This definitely makes the receiver feel very good, and the more beauty that happens to you is, you feel more powerful inside, which again increases your universal presence.

Environmental Presence Exercise:

"At least 3 times a day, 30 seconds each time connect to your environment".

Now that you have "Elevated your personal presence" and known the importance of Mind, Body and Environmental awareness, let's move to the next level. Step 2: Eliminate your Limiting Beliefs.

Step 2 - Eliminate your Limiting Beliefs

5 - Step Model To Reach Your Higher Consciousness

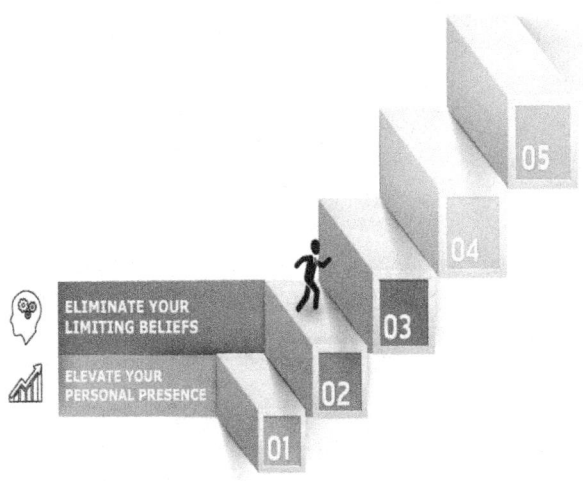

Chapter 3:
THE POWER OF BELIEFS

**"If you believe you can, or you believe you can't,
either way you are right"**
- *Henry Ford*

Once upon a time, a long time ago, there was a young man who lived in a small village. He owned three donkeys and used them to carry loads for people. One day, he was walking along a river towards his destination. The sun was at its peak, and it was a scorching hot day. The cold river water was tempting. He decided that he wanted to take a bath in the cold river water.

So, he started tying up his donkeys to the tree and realized that he only had 2 ropes enough to tie two of his donkeys. Of course, he can't leave the third donkey untied as it might wander away. So, he was perplexed. (This man had never left the donkeys untied even for a single day, and these 3 donkeys were used to being tied by the rope every day.)

When he looked around, he saw an old man (who looked wise) sitting under a banyan tree.

So, he walked over to the old man and asked, "Dear old man,

would you happen to have a rope that I can borrow."

The old man said, "I don't have a rope, but maybe I can help. What do you want the rope for?"

"It is so hot right now, and I have been walking for some time in this heat. I would like to take a dip in the cool river before I continue my journey. I have with me three donkeys. I have only two ropes to tie two of my donkeys to a tree, I don't have another rope to tie the third donkey. Now, I can't leave it untied as it might wander off and I can't afford that to happen. Hence, I wanted another rope so that I can tie the donkey and go for a dip in the river".

"This is easy," said the old man. "Just do the act of tying up the third donkey. Do everything you did to tie the other two donkeys and go for a dip in the river. Your donkey will not go anywhere".

"Really?" asked the young man.

"Believe me and do it," said the old man.

The young man walked away and decided to try what the old man asked him to do. He tied the third donkey with a virtual rope and went to take a dip in the river. He was apprehensive but still decided that the old man seemed wise and so decided to trust him.

When he came back from taking a bath, to his surprise and joy, he found that all the three donkeys were still there. So, he untied the two donkeys' and moved them. However, the third donkey did not move at all. He tried pushing, prodding and it didn't budge.

So, he went back to the old man and asked "The donkey that I tied as you requested me to is not moving at all. It is stuck. Can you please help?"

The old man asked him in return "Did you untie your donkey?"

The young man realized that he hadn't. So, he went back and

untied the virtual rope, and the donkey started to move again.

The young man thanked the old man and went ahead towards his destination happy and have learned some vital lessons.

The donkey thought it was tied up with the rope even though it wasn't, it believed it cannot move forward because the donkey was conditioned to be tied with a real rope every day. Today only the act of tying and removing the virtual rope made the donkey believe that it has been tied with real rope and it never tried to see if it really cannot move by moving. If it had decided to move forward, it could have quickly moved away from the place. This donkey was conditioned to a set of limiting belief.

Don't you think that human beings also have such limiting beliefs about themselves? Which stops them from moving forward in their lives? Before diving deep into limiting beliefs, let's find out what a Belief is? A simple definition of a Belief is-

"A Belief is an assumed truth with or without evidence."

In the above story, the donkey assumed that it has been really tied with a rope and hence cannot move. Here the donkey assumed the truth without the evidence (Donkey did not try to run).

Similarly, most of our beliefs that are formed in our lives are assumed to be right with or without any evidence. These are the beliefs that we inherit from our childhood through our own senses. Most of the ideas that are formed in us are based on our family, culture, religion, the society we live in. You find theists and atheists coexisting in a single society who all sometimes get into debates about their personal beliefs but eventually get over each other's differences and try to exist in harmony. These beliefs are formed based on the way that person has been brought up and the surroundings in which the person is exposed to, and a lot of it is affected by their education.

How do Beliefs get formed and what are their sources?

After completing my engineering, I was campus recruited and

joined one of the reputed IT companies in Bangalore. After around 2 years of working in IT, I had a desire to do an M.B.A from one of the top Ivy League Business Schools in the world. So, I started preparing for my GMAT exams. It was through GMAT exams that you could apply to all leading business schools in the world. As I started preparing for my exams, I had to manage both my work as well as my studies, and this was a great challenge for me.

The challenge was much higher for me because I was weak in verbal reasoning which comprised of reading comprehension, critical analysis, and sentence correction. I joined one of the coaching classes for GMAT, prepared day and night for around 3 months and then gave my first attempt in which **I scored 480 out of 800**, which was a pathetic score. With this score, there was no chance for me to get into any of the 3 tier Business schools, forget about Ivy League business schools. I was completely devastated. You need to have a score of at least 680 - 700 to have a chance of getting into Ivy League business schools. Then I joined another GMAT coaching class for 3 months and took another 3 more months to prepare myself thoroughly well for the exam. I gave many MOC and practice exams in which I scored well and was confident of doing well this time.

It was the day of my exam, **attempt no 2.** My score was 560. I was frustrated by seeing my score. I was not able to understand what was going wrong. I had prepared so well and was scoring more than 700 in practice exams. I was in a relaxed state of mind, calm and confident when I took my exam, even then I got only 560, I was not able to digest and find out the reason. By now in the last 1 year, I had already spent up to Rs 1 lakh (100000) for my exam and coaching classes and other study materials and books. But I was so desperate to do my M.B.A from top Ivy League Business schools that I decided to give it another attempt and crack it.

My attempt number 3: For my 3rd attempt I prepared for another 6 months and gave my exam. After completing my exam, I hit the finish button on my screen for the score to pop-up. I was keeping my fingers crossed, then when score showed up on screen, I could not believe what I saw on screen. For my 3rd attempt, I had prepared day and night for months. I slept only for 3-4 hours a day for months, and because of this, I developed Vertigo problem (Dizziness when I turn my head right side). After all these efforts I got a score which astonished me. My score was 550, which was less than my 2nd attempt.

I felt like killing myself.

Hit my leg hard on the exam table,

Pulled my hair extremely hard out of frustration,

Cried for some time and came back to my home. My parents consoled me and told me not to stress about it and that I have done my best.

Let me reveal you some vital points here: I was very poor in verbal reasoning which comprised of reading comprehension, critical reasoning, and sentence correction. And I was good in quantitative reasoning (Maths). Though I was not good initially in verbal reasoning, I had improved tremendously by working on my grammar, reading and comprehending skills and all other things needed for the exam.

The Ultimate reason what stopped me from scoring high marks was my LIMITING BELIEF:

"You are not good at English and can never improve."

In reality, I was just good enough in my English but not that great. Also, I used to hear often from parents of my friends that:

"Children studying in state syllabus schools are usually poor in English, and they can never improve."

And this limiting belief was set inside my subconscious mind without my knowledge. I realized about this limiting belief only after 2 years of my 3rd attempt during my transformation phase.

Just to give you a brief about schooling in India, we have

primarily 4 boards of school education, namely CBSE, ICSE, State boards, and IB. And each has its own advantage.

Though I studied very hard, improved my grammar, reading skills and my reasoning skills, my subconscious mind was always ruling my thoughts and was saying, "You are poor in English, and you can never improve because you are from state syllabus school." This limiting belief was the main reason why the result was not in my favor despite tremendous efforts.

Can you relate to this?

Can you just look back at your life and find out in any aspect of your life that though you had put in so much of efforts, the result was not in your favor? Maybe you have a limiting belief about yourself subconsciously which has caused you the opposite of the desired effect in a specific area of your life.

So, let's come to the source of beliefs.

For me, the source of my limiting belief was my friend's parents who also believed that children studying in state syllabus schools are weak in English and can never improve.

Most of the beliefs whether they are empowering, or disempowering beliefs are set at a very young age, usually until the age of 7. Beliefs are also set during interaction with people usually elders (parents, teachers, relatives, etc.). Due to the strong reasoning, the elders give, and we as young children are not mature enough and don't have the habit of questioning the reasoning, we believe the things said by our elders, and we assume that it is the truth and start living our lives thinking that is the truth. Some of these beliefs are transferred from one generation to another generation. As we get older, we change our ways of living. But the beliefs are so deep-rooted in the subconscious mind and remain unchanged. So, it is imperative to find out whether your beliefs are empowering you and helping you to move ahead and progress in your life or whether they are disempowering you and making you stick at the place where you are.

So, the significant portion of our beliefs come from our parents, elders, teachers, relatives, and friends. To put it in simple terms the source of these beliefs are from those people with whom we interacted and spent most of our time in our early childhood.

Another important source of belief is the major events that happened in our lives (can be at any age) which has created a profound impact. Some of these events can cause us to have limiting beliefs about ourselves, our lives and the world are:

➢ Separation from your loved one
➢ Accidents
➢ Chronic Illness
➢ Death
➢ Divorce
➢ Personal or Business failure
➢ Deep conversations between people
➢ Going into huge debt
➢ Constant criticism
➢ Conflicts and arguments at home or workplace

Above are some of the events which can cause limiting beliefs in you consciously or subconsciously. Also, you could have significant events that happened in your life which could have lead you to have empowering beliefs.

Some of the other sources of Beliefs are Society and its rules. The society has created many rules for us to live in. Some of the rules are dated as back as 2-3 generations. When we live in such kind of a social environment where we are told to follow the rules and live according to such regulations, we form certain beliefs and start living accordingly without bothering to know if these rules empower or disempower the progress in our lives.

Though we may question the rules of the society and feel they are not worth following any more as they stop my progress and freedom from what I desire, many still support the societal rules because there is something called as a human need, which is "Need to belong." We, humans, are the evolved species and love safety. You feel safe when you are in a group, and not when you are alone, hence we have this need to be accepted in a group or a society we live in. So, to be recognized in the community, we start following the rules irrespective of whether they empower or disempower us.

Importance of Self-Esteem

Let's see the importance of Self-Esteem (Self Belief) in our lives which can determine our actual progress. Also, let's see some examples of empowering and disempowering Self-beliefs that we can have consciously or subconsciously in our lives.

Self-Esteem beliefs are nothing but beliefs about yourself, your abilities, your capacities, your decisions, your emotions, and your behavior. It is a belief of your overall sense of self-worth or personal value. In other words, how much you appreciate and like yourself.

Empowering Self-esteem beliefs can play a significant role in your motivation and success throughout your life. Limiting or disempowering self-esteem beliefs may hold you back from succeeding at school or at work or in your life because you don't believe yourself enough to be capable of success. In contrast, having a healthy self-esteem belief can help you achieve big things because you navigate life with a positive, assertive attitude and believe you can accomplish your goals.

Limiting Self-Esteem beliefs are the most dangerous ones because

> **"You can never outperform your own self-image or self-worth"**

And most of your limiting self-esteem beliefs are subconscious beliefs, which you do not know you possess. This is the reason why limiting self-esteem beliefs are the most dangerous. These limiting self-beliefs can break you down and is very difficult to bounce back, and it requires a lot of time and conscious efforts.

I am telling this because I have experienced it myself. One of my biggest limiting Self-esteem belief was:

"I am not good enough."

And this one limiting self-esteem belief was enough which kept me live a mediocre life for 8 long years. It is essential that you recognize your limiting self-esteem beliefs so that you can remove it permanently and live a fulfilling life.

The first step in identifying your limiting self-beliefs is awareness of your thoughts. What kind of ideas you usually get when you try to do something new or when you are about to take some action towards your goal or when you sit to set your goals? You need to be aware of what are your first thoughts when you try to do some of these things. When you are aware only then you can identify your limiting beliefs and only then you can eliminate them. Hence you see Step 1 of this 5-step model – "Elevate your personal presence" is very important. Awareness is a critical element in finding any solution to a problem. Awareness helps you find more clarity to understand and take the required action in your life. So, first be aware of your thoughts, intentions, and emotions to find out what your limiting beliefs are.

Usually, most of the people say
Thoughts create feelings, then feelings create actions, then actions produce results.

Thought $\Longrightarrow$ Feelings $\Longrightarrow$ Actions $\Longrightarrow$ Results

But there is one more thing which creates Thoughts. Beliefs creates thoughts. You believe in something hence you think in that way and so does your emotions and feelings and so do your actions and results. So, you see it is your beliefs that create the effects in your life.

Beliefs $\longrightarrow$ Thoughts $\longrightarrow$ Feelings $\longrightarrow$ Actions $\longrightarrow$ Results

Below are some of the common limiting self-esteem beliefs most of the people have. Most of the limiting beliefs are deeply rooted in your subconscious mind. We first need to bring them out on the surface (Conscious level) through awareness.

Find out if you resonate with any of these.

1. I'm too old.

2. I'm too young.

3. I'm too poor ... I lack in having enough money and resources.

4. I'm too fat or too skinny ... too tall or too short.

5. I am not good enough

6. I'm not smart enough.

7. I'm not famous enough.

8. Others are in my way.

9. I can't start ... I'm not ready.

10. Wealthy people hold all the right cards.

11. Money is the root of all evil.

12. I'm a mess, it's hopeless.

13. I don't have enough time.

14. I don't have enough energy.

15. I can never be Financially free.

16. One day I'll change.

17. Exercise isn't that important.

18. My health is holding me back.

19. I'll never be happy.
20. Change is too hard.

21. Nice, faithful men (or women) are impossible to find.

22. I'll never be successful.

23. I just have bad luck.

24. I don't deserve nice things.

25. There's no point in dreaming big.

26. Others' approval is key to me feeling worthy.

27. I'll always be broke.

28. I don't have the right education.

29. Being honest leads to rejection.

30. I'm not important.

31. I'm not good with money.

32. I can't trust myself.

33. I'm unlovable.

34. I'm not self-disciplined.

35. There's no point in asking for what I want.

36. I'm powerless.

37. I am incapable of loving people.

38. I'm not strong enough.

39. I wasn't born into the right kind of family.

40. I don't have enough experience.

41. Why try? I'll just fail.

That's a pretty big list, so tell me, did you recognize yourself in any of these? Are there any other limiting self-beliefs not mentioned here that you noticed popping up in your self-talk?

"The key is to observe the thoughts that reveal your limiting beliefs."

All the above limiting self-esteem beliefs can be turned into empowering beliefs by just negating the above limiting beliefs. Let me show you few ideas from the above list.

I'm not strong enough -----------------> I am strong enough

I am not good enough ------------------> I am good enough

I am powerless ---------------> I am powerful

I'm not important ---------------> I am important

There's no point in dreaming big. ----------> Dreaming Big is the way to go in life.

Change is too hard -------> Change is easy and does not take time.

You got to know how you can turn a limiting self-belief statement into an empowering belief statement. When you add more empowering beliefs into your life, magic starts happening, and that's how you will manifest your desires in your life. Isn't that powerful? This is so powerful and yet so simple. When I began to identify my limiting beliefs and then later removed and installed empowering beliefs, my life changed at a faster rate than I had ever imagined. I was able to manifest most of the things in my life.

As you understand beliefs play a significant role in your life, you need to start adding more empowering beliefs into your conscious mind and then to your subconscious mind to create greater impact in people's life as well as yours. Many successful people in this world have achieved greater success because they had great self-esteem beliefs in them. To see the power of self-beliefs, let's look into these 3 examples of great people who achieved greatness because of their self-belief.

Invention of Aeroplane

One of the greatest devices that humans have ever witnessed. This is the story of two brothers (Wilbur and Orville Wright) who dared to believe that they could make humans fly. In the early 1900's everyone was trying to crack the puzzle that was controlled man flight. Everyone expected 'Samuel Pierpont Langley' will be the person to solve it first. Langley had the best team to work on, and he had all the funding required by the war department to develop the plane.

Whereas Wright Brothers looked like amateurs in comparison. Neither had gone to college. They had run a newspaper for many years, before opening a bicycle shop in 1892. They had little money, didn't know the right people, and no one paid them much attention. Yet, when they started studying the problems of human flight in 1897, they were sold. They believed human flight was possible and from that moment, decided to start experimenting themselves. When framed this way, not many would bet on the Wright Brothers to succeed, yet they had one intangible resource on their side: Strong Why (Purpose) and unshakable Self Belief (They believed in the idea of human flight so firmly that nothing would get in their way).

Langley made two attempts in 1903, both ending in terrible failures that led to much ridicule and fanfare. Nine days after Langley's second attempt, in Kitty Hawk, North Carolina, Wilbur, and Orville Wright made the first successful controlled human-crewed flight ever. The rest is history.

The Wright brothers accomplished the unbelievable because they dared to harness the power of belief and combine it with action.

The V8 Engine by Ford

The greatest motivator anywhere in the world has always been the power of belief. Henry Ford, the great Car Maker, was once trying to get an engine called V8 made. Now the V8 had some structural requirements which were considered impossible to be implemented practically. He told his team I am intelligent enough to understand that a V8 can be built, but only you people can build it because you have the skills. The employees told him, "you are our employer, and we can't argue with you, but it cannot be built. It is an impossibility." Ford said, go build it. 6 months went by, no luck, 8 months went by, no luck. A year went, and there were still no results. Finally, he said you don't come back until you have my engine because I know, and I firmly believe it is possible. I don't care how it is done, I just know it can be done. Guess what they finally found a solution and the V8 engine was actually built. Can you see the incredible power of belief?

The 4-minute mile by Roger Bannister

Before May 6th, 1954, no one in human history had run the mile in less than four minutes. Most people believed that this thing was physically impossible. A lot of so-called experts thought that it was beyond the capability of the human body to run the mile in such less time. In fact, they went on to say that a person who seriously attempted this feat would end up with lungs that can explode and certain death. For many years this belief was perceived as a fact, and during this period, a lot of athletes tried to break this barrier without any success.

However, a man named Roger Bannister, armed only with the power of self-belief and incredible determination, ran the mile in 3 minutes and 59 seconds on May 6th, 1954. By doing so he did not just create a world record, he also broke a false belief that existed in the minds of thousands of runners. To run a mile in less than 4 minutes was not possible. A year later many more people broke the barrier, and now this is commonplace. So, what does it mean? It means the wall never existed at all, it was just a barrier that existed in mind, not in nature! The "impossible was accomplished."

Do you see what the power of empowering self-beliefs can do to an individual or a company in a significant way?

Do you know what is your core empowering beliefs in your life?

Below are some of my core empowering beliefs that I live my life with.

1. You can never outperform your SELF IMAGE
2. Change small and change often.
3. Be congruent both inside and outside of you.
4. Why do you try all your life to fit in, when you are born to stand out?
5. Universe has everything in abundance, just ask for it, and you will be given.

These empowering beliefs enhance my progress as a human being and help me live my life with higher conscious levels with great energy.

How about you?

First, identify your limiting beliefs and eliminate them and then replace with empowering beliefs which will help you to move into your higher conscious levels with great energy.

Now that you saw the power of beliefs, next let's deep dive into how to find your limiting beliefs and steps to eliminate them and replace with empowering beliefs.

Are you Game?

KUMAR NAGENDRA

CHAPTER 4:

THE POWER OF CHANGING BELIEFS

"If you do not remove your limiting beliefs, you do not change your results in life"

Before you learn how to find your limiting beliefs, let's see what are the consequences of not identifying your self-limiting beliefs.

1. You paralyze yourself at the start line of something you want to do. You give excuses and convince yourself that you can't do this. With this, you don't give yourself an opportunity to try.
2. You will depend mainly on other people's opinion before you take a decision rather than depending on your own gut feelings and intuition. (Most of the self-limiting beliefs are based on other people's opinion and their own limitations. They are not your limitations, you just adopted them.)
3. You have a limited mindset which makes difficult for you to grow.
4. You are stuck in your same old emotions.
5. Your behavior patterns do not change and keep you in the same habit loop which does not enable you to move out of your comfort zone.
6. You will have difficulty in finding clarity in the things you

do.

7. More importantly, you will not have clarity in what's your real purpose of life.
8. You live your life on fear mode.
9. You will be mostly a follower and not a leader.

The above listed are only a few consequences.

So, can you imagine what it is to live with your limiting beliefs.?

Truly speaking

"LIMITING BELIEFS blocks your ABUNDANCE in all areas of your LIFE"

You saw earlier how my limiting belief "You are not good at English and can never improve" held me back from achieving a high score in my GMAT exam. This was a false belief I had which I assumed to be true subconsciously.

Most of our limiting self-beliefs are based on either fear or other people's opinions. As you can see my limiting self-belief was in other people's opinion.

Why do we Fear?

Human evolution is a million years of a process that has happened. For most of these years, humans were hunters and gatherers. As humans started to evolve so did our brain. The modern human brain has evolved from so-called old brain also known as the reptilian brain. The main characteristics of this old brain are survival instincts. Fight, flight or freeze response. So, when you are thrown out of your comfort zone, this brain senses danger and activates either of these 3 responses. You either fight or run away from the situation or sometimes freeze in a state of shock.

Humans by nature love to be in a safe and comfort zone. When we try to do something unknown, your brain pulls you back because you are entering an unknown territory which is out of your comfort zone. And most of us allow this fear to grow and will enable this fear to become a limiting belief subconsciously. And we keep nurturing this limiting belief, and it gets deep rooted inside of us, and then this limiting belief starts ruling our lives.

One of the ways to counter any of your fears and not scare your reptilian brain is to counter any of your limiting beliefs with the below powerful empowering belief consciously and consistently. As I said earlier this is one of my core empowering beliefs that I live with, and this has helped me tremendously.

"Change small and change often."

When you change small, you are not going too far out of your comfort zone, and you can quickly come back to your comfort zone if you feel scared or any danger. Once your brain knows this setup that you are not going too far out of your comfort zone, it allows you to play in the region which is just outside your comfort zone. After spending some time in this new territory, this new zone which you conquered becomes your comfort zone and thus expanding your comfort zone. When you take this strategy of change small and change often you can easily counter your fears and limiting beliefs.

This powerful strategy of change small and change often has helped me tremendously in countering my fear-based beliefs. Apply this same strategy in your life to counter your fear-based beliefs.

Now let's see what are the steps in which you can find out your limiting self-beliefs.

These were the same steps which helped me find my self-limiting beliefs. I have repeated this process many times to dig out my hidden limiting self-beliefs. At first, you may find it uncomfortable and hard to even think about your problems and reasons for those problems. This may put you a little just outside of your comfort zone. But you know

"The cave you fear to enter holds the treasure in it ".

So, are you committed to push yourself a little and dig out your hidden limiting self-beliefs?

Steps to find your Limiting Self-Beliefs

> *1. Choose a problem in any area of your life where you feel Stuck. It can be a money related problem, any health issues, relationship problems, personal or a professional problem. Just write down all the problems from every area of your life and make a list. Now from this list you decide which is the top priority one you need to address first.*

Now that you have selected a top priority problem, write this problem statement again on a fresh new page / sheet. For this exercise I recommend writing using paper and pen and not to use any devices / laptops. There is a reason behind it.

> *2. Get in touch with your thoughts and start writing down everything that comes to your mind about the problem at hand. You keep asking repeatedly:*
>
> *"Why I am having this problem?"*
>
> *Keep writing all the reasons why you feel you are having this problem. Write as many Why's for your problem until you have nothing left and your mind is quiet*

Important tips before you start the above Step2:

> Go to a quiet place to do this exercise.
> Before starting the exercise close your eyes for a minute and focus on your problem and have an intention saying, "Now I am going to find my limiting belief for this particular problem at hand."
> Keep a timer beside you. This is a timing exercise. Do not take more than 3-4 minutes.
> Do not overthink, if you take more time to write, your logical mind sets in. Lesser the time you give yourself to write, better will be your answers. Your reasons come from your subconscious mind.
> You must feel the emotions of your reasons when you write down without any judgment.
> Preferably you can play a soothing background music when you do this exercise. This is not compulsory.

To help you further in digging out your reasons (why?), you can look at the problem from a third-party point of view. Be the observer of your situation rather than a participant in it.

You can also use a powerful word "**because**" in digging out your reasons like below.

I am having this (problem) because

_____

Eg: I am not able to start a business because I don't have enough money.

I am not able to start a business because I don't have enough skills

I don't have enough skills because I am a slow learner

I don't have enough money because I don't have enough skills

Can you see there is a limiting belief? - *"I am a slow learner."*

This was just an example to show you how you can dig out your reasons and uncover your limiting beliefs. Just observe your first set of thoughts that come to you, and they will be the right reasons because they get generated from your subconscious mind.

> *3. Look back over what you wrote. Highlight every negative thought. You should see a pattern forming. Some of your negative thoughts may repeat and overlap. Most of the reasons or all the reasons you have found is a limiting belief.*

Note: When you write down the reasons make sure the reasons you give are not facts but a belief.

Facts are descriptions of reality. Beliefs are descriptions of our ideas about external reality.

Example 1: I am too fat because <u>I did not take care of my body and my eating habits.</u>

Example 2: I am not good enough because <u>everybody thinks so.</u>

Example 3: I am not successful because <u>I don't have enough resources.</u>

In the first example the reason given is a fact. "I did not take care of my body and my eating habits" is fact of the reality. Where as in example 2 and 3 the reason given is a belief. "Everybody thinks so" is a belief because it is your idea about external reality. Usage of strong and heavy words such as "Everybody", "Nobody", "Always", "Never" etc. indicates that it is your belief, your perception about a reality which may not be true.

"I don't have enough resources" is again a belief. Resources are there in plenty, it is just you need to learn to be more resourceful.

When you find a pattern of reasons for your problem, pick up the most repeating reasons as the priority or whichever the ones you feel it is important to eliminate first.

> *4. Final Step: Get a partner (your spouse or your friend with whom you can share comfortably) and read out loud your limiting beliefs and see how you feel as you read out loud. Observe your feelings and ask yourself whether do you really feel that this limiting belief is there in you?*

This final step is to confirm to yourself that yes, I have this limiting belief.

Having a partner will be useful. But if you don't find a partner do not worry, you can still do it all by yourself in front of the mirror.

So, these are the 4 steps using which you can find out your limiting beliefs. Let me share with you how I found my limiting self-belief "I am not good enough" by following the same above 4 steps.

My problems were:

- I was not able to start/take the initiative in any of the things that I wanted to do.
- Financially I was stagnant.
- I was not able to communicate appropriately with anyone.
- I didn't have a girlfriend

I am just listing some of the problems that I had for your reference. From the above list of the issues, I choose "I was not able to start/take the initiative in any of the things that I wanted to do" as the most priority problem to address first.

Then I sat down in silence, closed my eyes for a minute and thought about my problem at hand. And then for the next 4 minutes wrote down all the reasons why I am having this problem. Some of the reasons (My first few thoughts) I gave are:

- What if I cannot finish what I started, and I will feel disappointed and feel low.
- I am not good enough to do this. Already many smart people have done this and are highly successful.
- What will other people think of me, if I start doing this
- I will have to work very hard to accomplish this, and I must sacrifice many things if I start doing this.

I went on to find reasons for my next problem *"I was not able to communicate properly with anyone."* Below were some of my reasons

- I was afraid of even speaking normally (casually talking with one on one or with a group of people) with others because of my failure on stage while speaking in front of a huge crowd (Story explained in chapter 1: Personal Journey).
- What if I say something wrong while talking.
- I am not good enough in my communication skills due to my stage failure.

As you can see as I kept writing down the reasons why I am having this problem, I was able to dig out my limiting beliefs and bring them up to my conscious level and become aware of them. From the above reasons for my problems, I was able to see a pattern of belief that was being repeated, and that belief was "I am not good enough." Then as a part of the final step to confirm this belief indeed is true, I closed my eyes and shouted out loud my belief statement "I am not good enough" in front of the mirror and felt my emotions running through me which confirmed yes, I have this limiting belief in me.

This was a short glimpse of finding one of my limiting beliefs that I wanted to show you and make you understand doing this powerful exercise.

Now that you know the steps to find out your limiting beliefs, I highly recommend you take out some sheets of paper and a pen and do this exercise. Why procrastinate further in finding your limiting self-beliefs?

"TAKE ACTION NOW"

I recommend you do this for at least 2-3 problems and then try to eliminate your self-limiting beliefs because most of the time limiting self-beliefs repeat themselves in most of your questions in different areas of your life.

Next, let's learn how to eliminate your self-limiting beliefs.

Dear friend, the job is only half done now!!!

Steps to Eliminate your Limiting Self-Beliefs

> **1. Acknowledge your limiting Self-Beliefs and say "Thank you for being here with me on some purpose. Now I no longer require you."**

These limiting self-beliefs are also low vibrational energies present in you. It is important to acknowledge this energy because these low vibrational energies will be in a state of inertia. Upon admitting or acknowledging your limiting self-beliefs you are transferring some energy through your thoughts to these low vibrational energies and make them active so that it will become easy for you to eliminate.

> **2. Rate your belief from 1 - 10. How strongly do you believe about this limiting belief?**

You got to be real with yourself. Close your eyes, and you need to feel it from inside of you and rate yourself from a scale of 1 -10 how strongly you believe in this limiting self-belief. This step is not to know whether you have this limiting belief or not. Instead, this step is to find out how deep and intense is this limiting belief in you. Below are the few questions you can ask yourself which will help you rate this limiting self-belief.

-   Can you *absolutely know* whether this belief is true? Yes / No? If you are absolutely sure it is true you can rate high (7 - 10). If you feel *I might have this belief* but not very deep rooted, then you score accordingly say (4 – 6)
-   Have I always believed this belief or only sometimes?
-   How would my life be if I am not having this limiting belief?

---

3. Think, write down and visualize the consequences of holding onto your Limiting beliefs?

This step is significant. The objective of this step is to associate more pain in you if you hold on to this belief and do not eliminate it. First, think of what are all the consequences you will have in both short term as well as long term if you hold on to this belief. How not eliminating this belief can affect you physically, emotionally, financially and spiritually? Also, how can it change your relationships?

How will these make you feel?

Greater the pain you feel and visualize the same about the situations due to the limiting self-beliefs you will be more motivated to change. We humans always try to avoid pain and try to seek pleasure. So, think of all the consequences and pain you are undergoing and will undergo if you do not eliminate.

Feel the anger, frustration, experience the grief, regrets. Bring all your emotions to the surface and experience it to the fullest and allow yourself to cry if you want to.

4. Release your limiting beliefs to universe

Imagine and feel where in your body do you feel this energy of limiting belief. Give this energy color and shape. Say for example you can feel this energy of limiting belief at the center of your heart. Now give this energy a black/grey color. And give it a shape say a star. So, imagine a black color star at the center of your heart. You no longer require this energy of limiting belief. It's time for you to release it to the universe.

Now imagine you are pulling this black color star out of your body and releasing this star into the universe. And you see this black color star getting disappeared into the universe carrying your limiting self-belief. Now feel a sense of calmness inside you. All those negative emotions you had a few minutes back begin to fade away, and you start to feel your body getting lighter.

Now say "Thank you Universe for accepting my limiting beliefs in your realm."

5. Add Empowering Beliefs into your system

and strengthen them everyday

Write down as many empowering beliefs that you want to imbibe in your daily life and give reasons why you want to have these new empowering beliefs.

Say for example you just eliminated the belief "I am not good enough" and you replaced it with a new empowering belief "I am good enough and unique." Now give reasons why do you want to have this as your new empowering belief. Some of the reasons you can give are:

This new empowering belief "I am good enough and unique" will help me

- Move faster ahead to achieve my goals
- Change my life for the better.
- Feel good and inspired to take massive action.
- Believe in my capabilities and help me perform better.
- Try new things in life

Similarly, write down reasons for each of your new empowering beliefs that you have listed. The reasons may be the same or different for each of your new empowering beliefs but write it down as it is a determining sub-step which will help you start rewiring your brain with a new belief.

Now you must stand in front of the mirror and shout out loud each of your empowering beliefs 5 times. After you scream out loud each of your empowering beliefs takes a moment to observe how do you feel when you say out loud. You should feel more confident, more joyful and feel lighter.

Now to strengthen these empowering beliefs in your system, you can do the below everyday

- Read these new empowering beliefs every day morning as Affirmations / Declarations. It is by repetition these new beliefs will get strengthened.
- To make these new beliefs go into your subconscious mind, you can record your empowering beliefs in your mobile or any recording player for 10-15 mins by repeating it for as long as 15 mins and then listen to this recording while you go to sleep

or as soon as you get up in the morning every day. When you are about to sleep or as soon as you get up in the morning, you will be in alpha state (Not fully awake and not adequately rested). During this alpha state, you will have access to your subconscious mind easily.

- Engage with empowering people who are positive, action-oriented, result oriented and who have empowering beliefs, attitudes, and habits. By being around such people most of the time, you will take have positive energies from these people.

- Turn your affirmations/declarations into questions. Say one of your affirmation is "I am powerful and confident." Now turn this affirmation into question like this "How can I be more powerful and more confident?". Questions are more powerful than affirmations because they direct your mind towards finding solutions and help you take necessary action steps to solve your problems.

Now you have the powerful tool to eliminate your limiting beliefs and imbibe more powerful empowering beliefs in your life.

Only you and only you are responsible for this change to happen. Making the change happen is easy and does not take time. You need to be committed to making the change happen so that you have the fruitful results that you desired. And now is the time to change your limiting beliefs and move closer to your higher conscious level.

"Don't be in a state of inertia, TAKE ACTION NOW!"

STEP 3: EMBRACE MEDITATION

5 - Step Model To Reach Your Higher Consciousness

CHAPTER 5:

POWER OF MEDITATION – KNOW YOUR INNER CORE

"One of the major and most important ingredients that helped me and is helping me transform rapidly in my life is MEDITATION."

What made me Embrace Meditation?

When I was leading a Mediocre life for many years, I had no interest in any activities, I was most of the time lazy and spent time watching all the movies, tv shows and other unnecessary things which added no value to my growth. Financially I was stagnant, I had average health, no courage to do new things, less confident and many more problems.

One day while I was alone at home and watching tv and was surfing different channels, by chance I happened to watch one of the episodes by "BK Shivani from Brahma Kumaris on Meditation." This was the triggering point which lead to so many good things in my life. I joined their basic course and learned "Raj Yoga Meditation."

Practiced meditation for few months and then gave up meditation as it was boring.

After a few more months, I learned another form of meditation called "Transcendental Meditation." Practiced this form of meditation for 5 months and then again gave up doing meditation.

I was giving up meditation not because there was no improvement in me, in fact, there was lots of good changes and developments happening in me. I had no patience and was not consistent, I felt meditation boring and a waste of time just like many youngsters think. As I still lived a mediocre life and was not action oriented to develop personal attributes and imbibe specific values of excellence in my life.

But somewhere deep corner in my heart I felt I should take up meditation again and should not leave it as meditation had made me feel good and had increased my confidence levels.

They say once a trigger is established in your life, it leads you to so many different events, people and places. During this phase only, I found my mentor who helped me come out of my 8 years of self-confinement. Things started to fall in place, and I instilled many personal attributes and values of excellence and imbibed many different perspectives of life.

I had forgotten entirely about meditation for nearly 1 year. Then one day one of my friend Kiran, whom I knew for many years called me and invited for a meditation session at Taponagar (A highly natural energetic place where cosmic energies are stored). One must visit this place in his / her lifetime. This place is located on outskirts of Bangalore. After attending the session, I felt good, and I knew it was time for me to hold on to meditation as I had given up on it earlier.

Here I learned "Saptharishi Dhyana yoga meditation," and this time it was never looking back and not giving up. Now it's a journey of close to 3 years into regular meditation. I was consistent in my practice.

"Meditation is the most powerful tool you can find to enhance yourself in all core areas of your life."

I say this because I have experienced it and living it every day.

There are many different types of meditation, and each one of them is beautiful and liberating. Meditation is all about self-discovery and finding your real purpose of life and moving towards your higher conscious levels. You have to be consistent.

I feel so blessed and would like to thank the Universal Divine that I took up meditation as a daily practice in my life. My life started to transform rapidly.

As I always say, you must take care of all the 9 core areas of your life (You can learn this in my 2-day intensive signature program – **"Absolute Mind Champion – Unlock your Energies"**) and balance them. **Spiritual growth** is one among 9 core areas of your life, and I rate this among the top 3 areas of your life. It is that important if you want to move closer to your real purpose of life and accomplish it.

What exactly is Meditation? And why the silence?

"Meditation is all about silencing your Body, Mind, and Intellect."

Meditation is also about expanding your awareness and altering your state of consciousness. When you silence your body, mind, and intellect, many spiritual processes begin within you. This process of silence enables you to create channels of communication with higher powers and higher energies. Silence helps you deepen your awareness within. As you have seen in personal presence chapter, we deal with 2 types of presence, inner presence, and outer presence. To strengthen your inner awareness the best way is meditation.

If someone asks me why meditation? The answer I give to them is straightforward which is very powerful.

"Meditation helps you find your true purpose of life and helps you fulfill the same"

The next question people ask me is: *"Is Meditation the only way to find your true purpose of life?"*
My answer to this question is: *"NO."*

There are so many other ways also to find your real purpose in life. *But meditation is the best way to find your true purpose of life and much more beyond.* At least based on my personal experience, I can say this.

When you go in deep silence for some time, you can start listening to your inner voice much more evident than when you are awake consciously. Random thoughts keep coming when you are in profound silence, make no efforts to analyze these thoughts and let them go. As you keep practicing not to analyze your thoughts and just observe them, slowly your thoughts start to reduce and then you will be able to listen to your inner voice.

As mentioned earlier there are many different types of meditation that you can adopt. An approach of meditating may be different in various forms, but the primary objective (expanding your awareness) will remain the same. Below are some of the types of Meditation you can follow:

1. Mindfulness Meditation
2. Transcendental Meditation
3. Vipassana Meditation
4. Guided Visualization techniques
5. Saptarishi Dhyana Yoga Meditation
6. Sahaja Yoga Meditation
7. Raja Yoga Meditation
8. Sound Meditation

These are only some of them I have mentioned. I am not going to explain in detail as to how to do these meditations as that is not my objective here. My aim is to make you realize the importance of practicing meditation as a daily routine because the benefits that meditation can provide you are numerous and tremendous.

Below are 27 benefits of doing Meditation. Have categorized these benefits into 4 types.

- Physical Benefits
- Mental Benefits
- Emotional Benefits
- Spiritual Benefits

Physical Benefits

1. Reduces Stress (Reduces Cortisol - Stress producing hormone)

In this modern world and lifestyle, there is no escape from stress. External forces are more significant than your will power. If you do not take care of your internal wellbeing, then stress takes charge of your life, and stress will put your life in a deep mess. According to medical research, stress is the number one enemy of your health. Stress is the cause of at least 90% of all the diseases. Stress is a silent killer. When you are under stress, your body releases stress hormone called Cortisol, this hormone attacks and weakens your immune system, shrinks your brain tissues and opens the door for all types of diseases to set in. So, the best antidote for stress is Meditation. Meditation helps you to reduce your stress tremendously.

2. Enhances Good and Deep Sleep

There are millions of people who have difficulty in having proper sleep. Many of them are sleep deprived, many of them are suffering from insomnia and other sleep disorders. And this problem causes tiredness, and fatigue. To have a balanced life you need to have deep and quality sleep. Your body needs adequate rest and meditation helps you have a good, deep and quality sleep.

"Meditators are good Sleepers."

3. Strengthen Immunity

Meditation enhances your body to produce more antibodies and T-cells which acts as warriors to protect you from viruses, bacteria, and germs. Thus, meditation supercharges your immune system.

4. Enhances release of Endorphins, Serotonin, and Melatonin

Endorphins are responsible for a sense of happiness. The body uses this endorphin as an internal pain killer. Meditation helps you enhance this hormone called endorphin and enables you to elevate your feel-good factor. Joggers and runners also feel good after their workout because after you jog or run for some time, your body releases endorphins and makes you feel good and happy, and you experience a state of bliss. This wonderful mind-state is readily found through meditation.

Serotonins are neurotransmitters which help in relaying of signals from one part of the brain to another part of the brain. Serotonin chemical plays a significant role in enhancing your mood, which in turn contribute significantly to your overall state of wellbeing. And Meditation helps in improving the release of Serotonin in your body.

Melatonin hormone helps you have a restful sleep. And, this hormone melatonin is known to prevent cancer, strengthen the immune system, slow down aging, and has been linked to helping prevent over 100 different diseases. Meditation enables you to enhance this hormone, and you see the benefits. Isn't that tremendous?

5. Whole Brain Synchronization

Meditation helps you balance both left and right brain. The connectivity and communication between these 2 brains increase enormously which leads to whole brain synchronization. Meditation helps you to use both sides of your brain optimally. Otherwise, most of the people only use one side of the brain dominantly creating an imbalance.

Studies have shown that humanity's greatest philosophers, thinkers, inventors, and artists use both brain hemispheres together, in unison. Thus, Meditation is the key to whole brain synchronization.

6. Reduces headaches and muscle tensions

Meditation is the best way to relax your whole body from the tip of a toe to top of your head. Due to so many external factors imploding on you all the time, all your muscles get tensed and stressed, and you get headache especially when your muscles of your face, jaw, and neck are under pressure. As you sink in a meditative trance, all your muscles get released from the tensions caused and feel relaxed and fresh.

Mental Benefits

1. Improves Focus

For many years ~ (2 decades), the average attention span of humans has dropped from 12 seconds to 8 seconds which is less than the attention span of a goldfish (9 seconds). This is according to the research done. Due to the internet and the advancement of technology, devices, and too many distractions every day have caused us to lose our focus and concentration. We try to focus on too many things at a time instead of focusing on one thing at a time. Nowadays people believe doing multitasking is a cool thing. Initially, even I was mesmerized by doing multitasking, but later realized how it can affect our productivity by far means. It might seem like you are getting multiple things done at the same time, but what you are really doing is quickly shifting your attention and focus from one thing to the next. Switching from one task to another makes it difficult to tune out distractions and can cause mental blocks that can slow you down. Focus on one important thing at hand, finish it and then move to the next task. When you do tasks with laser-like focus, you will accomplish the tasks much quickly and easily. Meditation helps you enormously in improving your concentration and focus.

2. Improves Memory

Meditation enhances and helps you build a bigger and stronger Hippocampus area in your brain. Hippocampus is the most critical region for storing and retrieving information. This region can strengthen and grow new cells irrespective of your age. Bigger and stronger the hippocampus area in your brain, more significant is your memory. Meditation no doubt will help improve the memory of adults, but meditation can be a great tool especially for students in schools and colleges.

To share my experience and a small observation, before getting into a habit of meditation it was difficult for me to remember the 6-digit OTP bank passwords while doing internet banking, I had to see or read out the 6-digit numbers at least twice before entering them for authentication. Now after becoming a regular meditator I can easily remember the 6-digit OTP numbers at a glance and enter them without having to see or recall the numbers twice. Those 6 numbers smoothly flow out of my memory and make my net banking faster by a few seconds. This was one of the observations I have made concerning memory. This may sound silly but point to be noted for consideration.

3. Strengthens Self-Discipline and willpower

One of the major problems faced by most of the people is "Self-Discipline." Lack of self-discipline is the most significant barrier between you and your dreams and goals. And some of the primary or strong reasons why most of them lack self-discipline is they don't know their real purpose of life, they don't know what they are passionate about, they don't know what their limiting beliefs are and people expect instant results without having patience. And by embracing meditation, you gradually improve your self-discipline and so does your willpower improves. You also develop more patience and resilience which will help you to build stability within.

4. Enhances Mental clarity

By embracing meditation in my life, one of the most powerful benefits I have seen personally is "Clarity in whatever I do".

And there is a saying:

"CLARITY IS POWER"

This is absolutely true. Whenever I am about to take any decision, and I am very clear about making this decision I feel powerful. And all the decisions that I have taken where there was absolute clarity, the result was beneficial to me all the time. Embracing meditation can help you find clarity in the path you wish to travel.

Doesn't this make you feel powerful?

5. Enhances Mind Power

Embracing meditation increases your mind power tremendously. Your visualization power increases which in turn helps you connect and trigger new neurons pathways in your brain. Your ability increases **MULTIFOLD** to analyze, comprehend and respond in your daily life in a better way. You will be more receptive to higher energies and higher knowledge when you embrace meditation.

You will develop a **"Warrior Attitude"** which will help you in challenging situations in your life.

6. Improves Creativity

You need to have a synchronized brain to be creative. You need to have more connections between neurons to be creative. When more connections are happening between your left brain and right brain the chances of being more creative are high. This can occur when the area "corpus callosum" is supercharged. This area is supercharged easily by embracing Meditation.

7. Brings Peace and calmness

The ultimate thing all humans crave is Peace of mind. Isn't it? What better way than embracing meditation to have peace of mind. As I said earlier and keep saying it repeatedly: "The external forces and noises are greater than our willpower." So, it is essential to remain calm and at peace internally even though lots of noises keep screaming at us. Only when you are more focused, have clarity in what you do and know your real purpose and passion, you can keep all those noise and distractions at bay. For this to happen first, you need to be calm, and at peace from within only then, you will be able to radiate the same attributes outside also.

"It's always inside out and not the other way."

Emotional Benefits

1. Control of Anger

Anger is one of the most potent destruction causing negative emotion, which humans have. Very few know how to use Anger for a constructive purpose. Violence has created lots of disruption in people's lives in terms of relationship, finance, health, and career. Anger is a phenomenon where your intelligence and logical mind is at its low and your emotional mind at its peak. In such situations, people tend to lose control of what they are saying and thinking, and they cause damage to the specific areas of their life. And this, in turn, leads to many other problems.

To control anger, you must first become aware when you get angry. Unless you are aware how can you manage it? Embracing meditation will help you become aware and control your anger and enables you to remind yourself to radiate more love to others.

To share my experience in this regard, by nature I don't get angry quickly. Whenever I used to get angry, I use to carry that anger for many days and suffer internally, and most of the time I used to be angry at myself for not doing certain things which I had intended to do in time. But after embracing meditation into my life, whenever I get angry with myself or others, I immediately become aware of my anger consciously before my irrational brain sets in and directly talk to myself and remind myself to radiate more love and not hate. This quick self-talk internally calms you down and allows your logical mind to set in. The only way to achieve this is through meditation and practicing it daily.

2. Overcome Anxiety and depression

Embracing meditation is the best tonic for overcoming anxiety and depression. Meditation helps release more serotonin in the brain which allows you to overcome anxiety and depression.

3. Enhances Happiness and Joy

Happiness and Joy are the two innate qualities of a human being but also the most forgotten ones. Due to obsessive thoughts and negative factors controlling your mind, we have forgotten to tune inwards and lost the natural ability to be happy and joyful. Embracing meditation helps you reset your happiness within and thus turning you into a more joyful person.

"Meditation has made me realize that being happy and joyful from within you can achieve anything you want."

4. Enhances better relationships

Embracing meditation helps you open up in all areas of your life more importantly in your personal relationships. Meditation enables you to let go off and allows you to forgive others because the main essence of meditation is pure love and silence. You will realize how easy it is to break the wall that you have built around people and be more open to receive and give love and care.

5. Overcome Fear

Everyone has experienced fear, including you and me. Humans have a primitive fear center in the brain called "Amygdala" which activates fear inside us whenever we are exposed to any danger, bad news or adverse circumstances. Due to constant external negative factors bombarding us daily, this fear center is most of the time active and functioning in full capacity which is the main reason most of the people do not take actions in their lives.

According to neuro scientists and meditation researchers by embracing meditation you can deactivate this region in your brain. By practicing meditation regularly, the electrical activities in the amygdala region are almost nil.

6. Enhances Emotional Intelligence

Embracing meditation enhances your emotional intelligence multifold. You are more aware of your emotions and thoughts. You have a balanced emotion, and you do not allow your feelings to go to the extremes. You can better access other people's emotions also and guide them better. And helps you remove emotional baggage that you are carrying from many years if at all.

Spiritual Benefits

1. Activates and balances your Chakras (Human energy centers)

The primary energy centers of humans are called Chakras, and there are 7 main such energy centers in our system. It's essential that these 7 chakras are activated and are in balance to have limitless abundance in all areas of your life. Embracing meditation is the best method to activate and balance your chakras. You will be learning in detail about the chakras in the next step: Energize your energy centers.

2. Expands your Aura

As how the earth has a magnetic field around it to protect from harmful rays, so do we humans have an electromagnetic energy field surrounding us known as Aura. Your Aura forms your personal energy space. Embracing meditation helps you strengthen and expand your Aura which enables you to experience higher dimensions of life. You will be learning in detail about the Aura in the next step: Energize your energy centers.

3. Awakens your Intuition power

One of the most valuable thing a human have is the power of Intuition. Most of the people hardly use it, and a very few use intuition to the fullest. Intuition helps you make better decisions in your life which in turn enables you to become successful in what you choose to do.

Embracing meditation strengthens the power of intuition within and allows you to make those powerful, courageous and crucial decision of your life. Some of the great and successful people who were very intuitive in their decision making were Bill Gates, Warren Buffett, Steve Jobs, Richard Branson, Albert Einstein and many more. You can also become part of this list of great intuitive successful people in the future if you can also make use of your intuition power to the fullest. The choice is yours.

4. Enables Higher Consciousness

Embracing meditation nourishes your consciousness to the highest level, which helps you live in this moment and makes you realize the most important thing in your life –

"You are ALIVE." This one realization or thought is sufficient to put yourself into a higher conscious level, and meditation helps you achieve this higher conscious level.

5. Become Oneness with the Universe

The universe is one infinite consciousness in which we live. Every living and non-living thing is part of this one big consciousness the universe. When we go beyond our mind, intellect and ego we can experience oneness with the universe and meditation can help you experience this wonderful experience of unity with the universe. When your thoughts completely fade away while you are meditating, and you slip into the awareness of being one with the universe, you feel the joy and bliss of being one with this consciousness.

6. Discover your true-life purpose

Through meditation, you can find the real purpose of your life. You can find your life's real meaning only when you connect yourself from within. You need to become aware of your thoughts and emotions to the deepest level from within. You need to listen to the answers what is within you when you are entirely in still and silence in meditation.

7. Experience the Light (Universal White light)

Embracing meditation helps you experience the universal white light which is the source of all creation. We can use this white light to channel through us and radiate and heal the entire planet earth and all its living and non-living things. This light is one of the purest forms of energy you can receive from the universe and meditation helps you have this energy.

8. Cleansing and Healing of the system

Meditation helps you cleanse and heal your entire body. Meditation has healing powers when used effectively can help you heal your problems and helps you come out of the problem with strength and confidence. When you are unwell, you can meditate and heal your illness faster along with your medicines. Meditation acts as a catalyst in recovering from your illness.

Thus, you see, embracing meditation in your life regularly can help you in many aspects of your life and help you bring out your real potential in use. As we saw the benefits, let's also see some of the misconceptions people have about meditation.

Misconceptions about Meditation

1. Meditation does not mean running away from your normal life, your problems and your responsibility. It is not going away from your home and families and be alone in a quiet place. Instead, meditation helps you lead a

quality life, face all your problems confidently and helps you take greater responsibility in your life with high self-esteem.

2. Meditation is not for youngsters, and it is only for old and retired people. This again is a significant misconception among younger people. Meditation brings you awareness and helps you know yourself from within. So, what if you are young or old, it doesn't matter as long as you have the urge to grow personally. The more the urge you have at a younger age to grow better, it is good for yourself and the world. And what better way to grow than embracing meditation. Based on my observation it's good to see many youngsters embracing meditation in their life's. So, anyone above 6 years of age can adopt meditation.

3. Only Meditation is enough, and nothing else is required is another misconception people are having. If I keep meditating, the universe or God will give me everything. This kind of thought will add only misery in your life because you kept expecting everything from the world without taking any ACTION in your life. Meditation will help you open the doors of happiness, joy, love and many opportunities in your life. You must walk in that door and make a conscious effort to change, take required actions to grow and learn and transform yourself to be a better version of yourself every day. Taking action is the key along with meditation.

4. Meditation is religious, and that's the reason I don't want to embrace it. Meditation is all about exploring yourself at the deepest level. How knowing yourself can become religious? Meditation is a powerful tool for all humans on this earth irrespective of what your religious views are.

5. Meditation is only about relaxing. Meditation is not only about relaxing, you have already seen so many benefits you can have by embracing meditation. It is a way to move into your higher conscious levels. Meditation is a way to connect to higher powers of universe. Meditation

is a way to have inner peace and inner strength. Meditation is a way to heal yourself.

6. Meditation will give you instant results is again a misconception. You are going to get the results you want if you practice consistently. How fast you achieve the results still depends on at what level of energy frequency you are vibrating in your life. It also depends on what sadhanas you have done in your life. It depends on the purity of your thoughts and intentions and many other factors. Yes, if you have all these and vibrating at these specific energy frequencies, you can instantly achieve the results you want. But to reach this level, you must do lots of sadhana, and for this, you need to have patience and faith. Most of the people lose patience and faith and hence quit doing meditation in between and therefore do not achieve their required results. There will be lots of obstacles in your path, you must go through them patiently and become more resilient and strong in your life.

Embracing meditation has given many benefits to millions of people. Embracing meditation has given me a beautiful and quality life that I wanted to live, and I have been living every moment of my life with happiness, joy, and love.

When millions of people are getting benefited including me, why not you also get all the benefits and energies by embracing meditation in your life?

I am not going to teach you any specific type of meditation here as my objective here was to make you realize the importance of embracing meditation. There are many types of meditation you can adopt. Adopt any one kind of meditation and follow it consistently and have faith and patience. You will definitely transform your life to the highest level.

So, will you embrace meditation in your life?

STEP 4: ENERGIZE YOUR ENERGY CENTERS

5 - Step Model To Reach Your Higher Consciousness

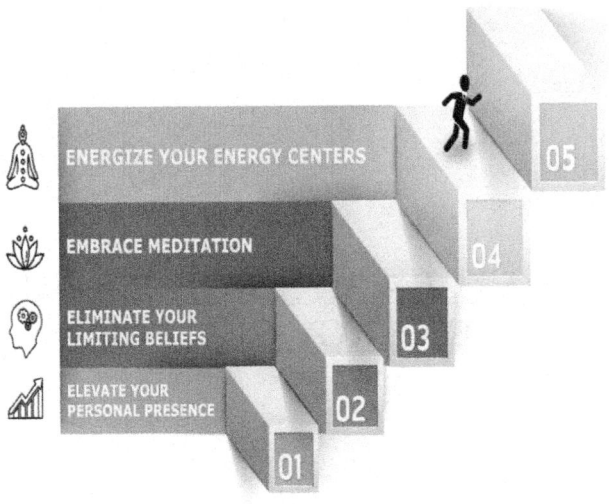

CHAPTER 6:

POWER OF ENERGY AWARENESS

"Everything is Energy and Energy is Everything"

Everything in this universe is energy and to move to your higher conscious levels, it is essential to be aware of your energies inside you and surrounding you.

Most of the people are ignorant and neglect the study and importance of energies. Energies cannot be seen but play a significant role in our lives. Lack of awareness about energies has created lots of problems and imbalances in the human system.

Why are people ignorant about energies?

A simple answer to this question would be a lack of awareness and lack of understanding of energies.

So, my next question would be why is there lack of awareness about energies?

The answer to this question could be a few reasons such as
- **Lack of subject matter experts** (not many people are spreading this knowledge of energies to others).

91

- **Lack of belief** (people do not believe in such existence of energies as they cannot see it through their naked eyes).
- **Lack of using Intuition** (people think only in logic and do not try to use their in-built capabilities such as intuition).

As I kept saying previously in this book and I keep saying it again and again that "**AWARENESS**" is the essential step and first step towards anything that you want to manifest in any area of your life. So, let's become aware of the energies and learn about them so that you can make the best use of the energies both inside and outside of you in your life.

So, what is Energy?

As in school books that we have learned, "Energy is the capacity to do work." This is one of my favorite questions that I ask my participants in my signature program *"Absolute Mind Champion - Unlock your Energies."* Most of the time the first answer I get is "Energy is the capacity/ability to do work." I ask what else energy is? Then I start getting answers like there are different forms of energy such as

Kinetic energy, potential energy, Chemical energy, Thermal energy, Electrical energy, Gravitational energy, Sound energy, Nuclear energy, Light energy, and people also tell about sources of energy like renewable and non-renewable energies. All these are correct answers, but these are not the answers that I seek.

Some people who have awareness about energies give me better answers such as thoughts and intentions are also energies, your emotions are also energies. All the living and nonliving things around you is energy vibrating at different frequencies.

The entire creation in this cosmos is energy, and this energy has the intelligence to manifest itself in different forms across different planes in this universe. At the beginning of the creation of the universe, a special energy in the form of sound was introduced at various points in the cosmos. This sound energy initiated the movement at various points and creation started to happen in the form of billions of galaxies, billions of stars and planets. So, all the matter at its fundamental level is energy including our human body. It is essential for us to understand how the human energy system works and using these energies from human plane and 6 different higher planes how you can make your life more beautiful and abundant both **spiritually** and **materialistically**.

This is just a gist about energies, and this subject of energy and cosmos is so vast and can be studied in depth, and it's just so fascinating to know about the universe, existence of life and so on. But here in this chapter, we will learn about human energy centers and the human energy field.

As you know everything in this universe is energy, let's try to understand the connectivity between Body, Mind, and Soul.

The body, mind and soul, each are energies vibrating at different frequencies. Every energy vibrating at different frequencies have various forms. For example, Earth has a rate of about 10 Hz - 13 Hz. Hence earth is very dense in its nature. Lower the frequency the thicker is the form.

Your body is physical and is visible and vibrates at a lower frequency. Your mind vibrates at mid-range frequency and soul vibrates at higher range frequency, and hence both mind and soul are invisible for a human eye. All these frequencies are measured using Brainwave activities.

As Earth has a Magnetic field around it, we humans also have an energy field around us called AURA.

Just how magnetosphere and ionosphere shield the planet earth from harmful radiations, Human AURA also protects us from harmful energies entering us. We have 7 layers of energy bodies surrounding the physical body, which will be in the shape of an egg arranged concentrically around the physical body. These energy bodies are arranged as shown in the diagram.

Diagram - Chakras and energy bodies

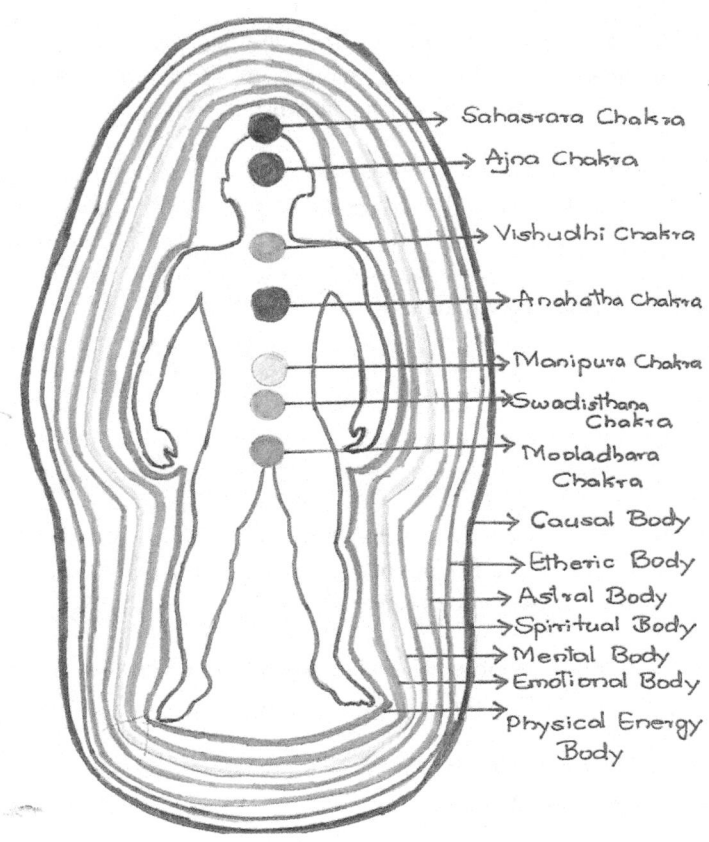

→ Sahasrara Chakra

→ Ajna Chakra

→ Vishudhi Chakra

→ Anahatha Chakra

→ Manipura Chakra

→ Swadisthana Chakra

→ Mooladbara Chakra

→ Causal Body

→ Etheric Body

→ Astral Body

→ Spiritual Body

→ Mental Body

→ Emotional Body

→ Physical Energy Body

As we have physical organs like eyes, brain, lungs, etc., supporting the physical body, we also have human energy centers known as chakras working as organs for the energy bodies. When a person is alive and healthy, these energy centers (Chakras) and energy bodies have to be harmonious and well balanced. These chakras produce an energy field around the physical body as well as the energy bodies, known as AURA. The Aura will also be in shape of an egg.

There are 7 main chakras in humans and they are

1. **Mooladhara Chakra** (Root Chakra) - This chakra vibrates with Red color frequency and is located at base of your spine near the cervix region.
2. **Swadhisthana Chakra** (Sacral Chakra) - This chakra vibrates with Orange color frequency and is located between sex organ and navel point.
3. **Manipura Chakra** (Solar Plexus Chakra) - This chakra vibrates with yellow color frequency and is located at navel region.
4. **Anahata Chakra** (Heart Chakra) - This chakra vibrates with green color frequency and is located at center of the heart region.
5. **Vishuddhi Chakra** (Throat Chakra) - This chakra vibrates with light blue color frequency and is located at the throat region.
6. **Ajna Chakra** (Third eye chakra) - This chakra vibrates with indigo color frequency and is located between 2 eyebrows in your forehead.
7. **Sahasrara Chakra** (Crown Chakra) - This chakra vibrates with violet color frequency and is located at the top of your head.

And each of these chakras produce its respective energy bodies around the physical body. The 7 layers of energy bodies are

1. **Physical energy body** (1st layer) which emerges from Mooladhara chakra.
2. **Emotional energy body** (2nd layer) which emerges from Swadhisthana chakra.

3. **Mental energy body** (3rd layer) which emerges from Manipura chakra.
4. **Spiritual energy body** (4th layer) which emerges from Anahata chakra.
5. **Astral energy body** (5th layer) which emerges from Vishuddhi chakra.
6. **Etheric energy body** (6th layer) which emerges from Ajna chakra.
7. **Causal energy body** (7th layer) which emerges from Sahasrara chakra.

As I mentioned your Aura also emerges from your chakras. The condition of your chakras (whether they are blocked, opened, overactive or balanced) determines the health of your Aura. The bigger and healthier your aura you will attract more positivity and abundance in your life.

Below are 2 diagrams that represent healthy and sick aura.

Diagram - Healthy Aura

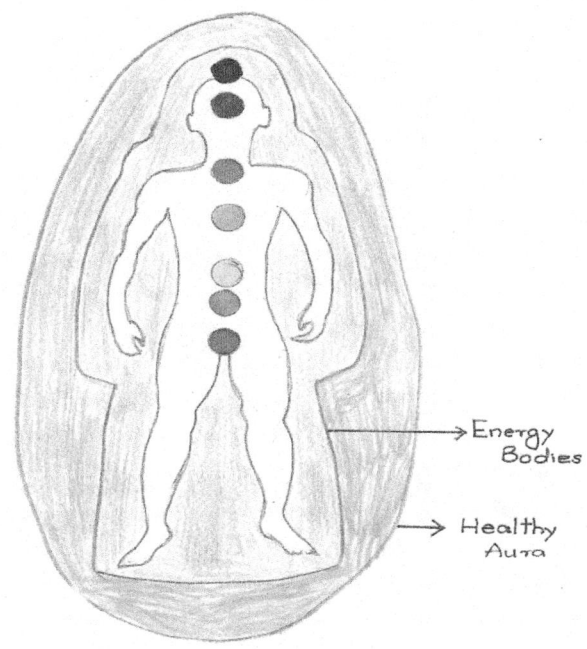

→ Energy
   Bodies

→ Healthy
   Aura

Powerful and Healthy Aura

Diagram - Sick Aura

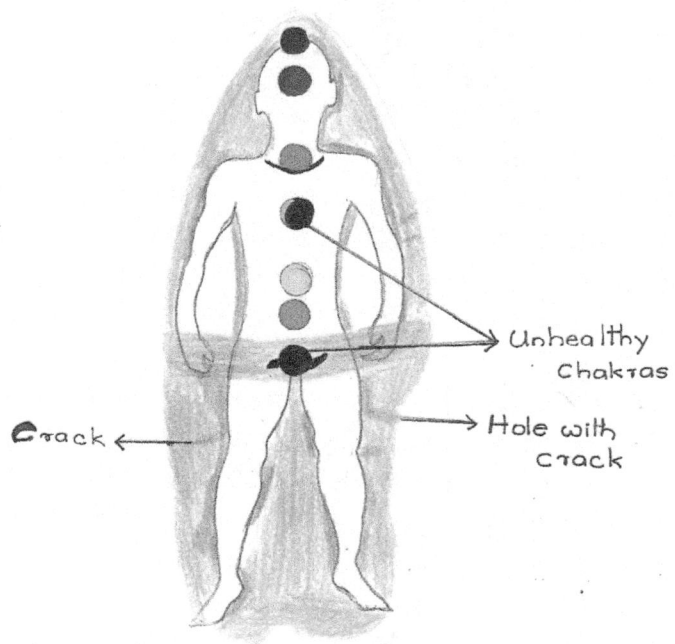

Sick Aura

The human aura extends out several feet around the body. Your character tells a lot about you – like whether you are tired, happy, friendly, logical, emotional, depressed, etc. It's like reading a map of energy. Your Aura acts like your energetic space. The bigger and stronger your aura, it will be more difficult for low vibrating energies to penetrate inside your energy centers. In simple terms, you will hardly attract negativity, negative people and adverse situations in your life and you will be most of the time vibrating at higher frequency energies and attract beautiful people, beautiful opportunities and fantastic experience for yourself. That's how powerful your aura and chakras are.

The amplitude and frequency of each Chakras output determine the size and shape of your AURA. The beliefs you develop in your human experience can alter the size, and shape of your chakras and hence changing the size and shape of your AURA.

To make your aura and chakras work more effectively and make it active, balanced and healthy, it is vital for you to first understand the characteristics of each chakra. What happens when each of your chakras is blocked, what happens when each of your chakras is overactive or underactive and what are the implications of these at a physical and emotional level.

So, before we begin learning the characteristics of each chakra lets understand from where these energy centers originate. Will explain you in short, and this answer is nonscientific and may appear to you illogical. You may believe it or not, it is up to you.

When this cosmos was created, there was also the creation of 14 different planes (Lokas). The first 7 planes (Lokas) are called Higher planes (Higher Lokas), and the remaining 7 planes are called lower planes (Lower Lokas). The activities in higher planes are spiritual. Spirituality was maximum in the most upper plane (Loka), and spirituality decreased gradually downwards. The activities in the lower planes (Lokas) was material, and it increased downwards, being maximum at the lowest plane (Loka). Our earth belongs to the 7th plane (Bhu Loka) where both spiritual and material activities are equal. Here in this earth (human) plane both good and evil has equal opportunities. Just to give you information of the names of these 14 planes (Lokas), the higher planes are Satya Loka, Tapo loka, Jana Loka, Maha Loka, Suva Loka, Bhuva Loka and Bhu Loka (Earth). The lower planes are Atala, Vitala, Sutala, Rasatala, Talatala, Mahatala and Patala Lokas.

When souls decided to take birth on planet earth (7th plane), souls had to pass through the higher 6 planes to enter our earth plane. At the beginning of the soul journey, each soul will be given mental sheaths that will be required to experience life in cosmos. As the souls enter each plane, a gadget was attached to their mental sheaths to mark their entry into that plane and also help them connect to that plane and draw energies. This gadget is what is known as Chakra. Hence, we humans have 7 major chakras (energy centers), 6 chakras from higher six planes and the 7th chakra (Mooladhara chakra) from the earth plane.

So, in simple terms what is Chakra?

Chakras are the openings to higher consciousness. They are the entrance through which emotional, mental and spiritual energy force flows into physical expression.

There are basically 114 chakras in our Human system. These 114 chakras are energy junction points which connects 72,000 Nadis in our human system. Out of these 114 chakras, the most important are 7 major chakras which are aligned across your spinal cord in a straight line.

Let us keep this information in mind and proceed ahead to learn the characteristics of each of these 7 major chakras.

Diagram – 7 Major Chakras

1st Chakra - <u>MOOLADHARA CHAKRA (ROOT CHAKRA)</u>

This chakra is located at the very base of your spine, near your tailbone and the color it vibrates is ***<u>RED</u>***

Symbol: 4 petals and sound frequency is "LAM."

Characteristics of Mooladhara Chakra (Root Chakra)

The Mooladhara chakra is the first chakra. Its energy is based on the earth element. It's associated with security, safety, stability, grounding and basic needs such as food, sleep, shelter, etc.

It's at the base of the chakra system and lays the foundation for expansion in your life.

The root chakra provides the foundation on which we build our life. It supports us in growing and feeling safe and helps us to explore all the aspects of life. It is related to our feeling of safety and security, whether it's physical or financial safety. To sum it up, root chakra is where we ground ourselves into the earth and draw energies from the earth and manifest the material things in our life.

This chakra is also associated with your adrenal glands, large intestine, bones, your legs, and feet.

What happens when this chakra is BLOCKED or IMBALANCED?

- You feel stressed about your finances. Money does not flow smoothly to you.
- You feel insecure and nervous.
- You become more defensive and procrastinate.
- Fear overtakes you in all areas of your life.
- Weak immune system

What happens when this chakra is OVERACTIVE?

- You will be more greedy
- You will feel more negativity.
- You will have Eating disorders

What happens when this chakra is OPEN or BALANCED?

- You feel safe and fearless.
- Money smoothly flows to you.

- You are more connected to earth and have more physical stability.
- You will have good immune and digestive system.
- Good health and have more patience

How to balance or energize this chakra?

What does the balancing of a chakra mean? This means the proper amount of energy flows into this chakra which helps in keeping all the physical and emotional systems in its optimal condition and work accordingly. Either more energy flowing or less energy flowing will cause an imbalance in the human system and hence it is best to balance the energy as much as it is required.

You can always analyze your life at present and look out for symptoms whether your Mooladhara chakra is balanced, imbalanced or overactive.

Some of the ways to balance this chakra.

To balance this chakra, you need to be more connected with earth energy. For this to happen, you can do various activities such as spend more time in nature, gardening, etc. Have more physical activities such as walking, jogging and doing Yoga helps you balance this energy.

Cleaning your place often with your own hands. Declutter your room, table, wardrobes, living space, kitchen, office room, and office tables, etc. When you do these activities, you are always connected with the earth element, and hence you can strengthen your Mooladhara chakra.

If you have an overactive Mooladhara chakra, you can practice more of kindness and compassion so that your energy will get balanced out.

You always have the best tool to balance this chakra. Yes, it's MEDITATION. You can close your eyes and focus on this chakra at the base of your spine for several minutes.

You can also balance this energy by eating foods that are grown under the earth such as carrots, beetroots, potatoes, radish, etc.

Just being aware of this chakra and setting an intention with a thought every day that my Mooladhara chakra is active and well balanced helps the energy to flow fluently at this energy center.

2nd Chakra - SWADHISTHANA CHAKRA (SACRAL CHAKRA)

This chakra is located between your navel point, and sex organ and the color it vibrates is **ORANGE**

Symbol: 6 petals and sound frequency is "**VAM**"

Characteristics of SWADHISTHANA Chakra (Sacral Chakra)

Swadhisthana chakra energy is based on water element, and its power is characterized by flow and flexibility. So, this chakra helps you to be flexible in life. The function of the sacral chakra is directed by the principle of pleasure. It is the basis of your sexuality and sensuality. All your sexual desires arise from this energy center. This chakra also governs your emotions as it is associated with emotional energy body. This chakra energy helps you bring out the inner child in you and enables you to experience joy.

This chakra is the driving force for the enjoyment of life through the senses, whether it's auditory, through taste, touch, or sight. When you have strong Swadhisthana chakra, it allows you to "feel" the world around and in us.

Another essential characteristic of this chakra is Creativity. This chakra helps you in being a creative person.

Parts of the body associated with this chakra are the lower abdomen, kidneys, bladder, sexual organs, circulatory system.

What happens when this chakra is BLOCKED or IMBALANCED?

- You will have emotional problems. Your emotions will rule rather than you rule the emotions. You may feel stuck in a feeling or mood for a long time and will find it difficult to come out of that emotion.
- You may have sexual and reproductive problems and may face urinary and kidney dysfunctions.
- You may not feel the joy and happiness from within as you lack the power to express your feelings and emotions.
- You may also face depression and lack passion and creativity.

What happens when this chakra is OVERACTIVE?
- You may overindulge in fantasies and sexual obsession.
- You become an addict to certain pleasures such as food, different forms of entertainment, drugs, etc. You start to over enjoy things which may not be suitable for your health or society.
- You may face obesity, hormonal imbalance, and restlessness.

What happens when this chakra is OPEN or BALANCED?

- You will be more committed in your life with the decisions you make in life.
- You will be more passionate and more creative in nature.
- You will be in control of your emotions and will not take decisions emotionally.
- You will enjoy your life to the fullest and experience the beauty of life and nature through your senses.
- You will experience intimacy and love freely and fully.

How to balance or energize this Swadhisthana chakra?

- You have to let go of the unwanted emotions that you are holding on to for a long time. Forgive someone or yourself from the bottom of your heart so that you let go of those emotions that are draining your energy apart.
- As this chakra vibrates that of orange color, eating foods orange/yellow in color helps you balance this energy. Foods such as honey, almonds, oranges, pumpkins, carrots, etc.
- Spending time watching lakes, rivers, streams, and oceans help you balance this energy.
- Elevating your personal presence (Step 1) will help you balance this chakra energy. Just being aware of this chakra and setting an intention with a thought every day that my Swadhisthana chakra is active and well balanced helps the energy to flow fluently at this energy center.
- Different yoga poses or asanas such as Virasana, Utkata Konasana, Virabhadrasana, Mandukasana, and many

more asanas will help you increase the energy in this center.

The best tool – Meditation

You can close your eyes and start focusing on this chakra point region for several minutes.

3rd Chakra - MANIPURA CHAKRA (SOLAR PLEXUS CHAKRA)

This chakra is located exactly at your navel point and the color it vibrates is *YELLOW*

Symbol: A circle with 10 petals in which is inscribed a downward-pointing triangle and sound frequency is "RAM"

Characteristics of MANIPURA Chakra (Solar Plexus Chakra)

Manipura Chakra energy is based on the Fire element. The main feature of this chakra is **PERSONAL POWER**. This chakra governs your will power, taking responsibility for one's life, personal identity, self-confidence, and self-esteem. This chakra enables you to take actions in your life confidently.

Have you been in a situation where you have taken decisions based on your gut feelings? You might have known that "Yes" this is absolutely right for me and I need to go for it. And where do you feel the sensations in your body when taking such gut decisions? Your stomach area, right? If you harness the Manipura chakra energy properly, you will often make those gut feeling decisions easily.

This chakra gives you the transformative power to change for good.

When this chakra vibrates with higher levels, it gives the person an abundance of wisdom to lead life.

It also helps a person to find his or her purpose of life and shows a direction to move forward.

Parts of the body associated with this chakra are a digestive system, pancreas, your muscles, and adrenals.

What happens when this chakra is BLOCKED or IMBALANCED?

- You may have a feeling of helplessness and irresponsibility.
- You will lack self-confidence and have low self-esteem which creates an impact on your social life.
- You may find other people taking control over your life, and you feel powerless and often feel rejected.
- You will have a lack of direction and purpose, and you will just go about your life without any plans and goals.
- Sensitive to criticisms.
- You may face physical problems such as digestive disorders, high blood pressure, diabetes, fatigue, and

pancreatic issues.

What happens when this chakra is OVERACTIVE?

- You have excessive control and authority over other people and situations which may not be useful to your relationship.
- You may start misusing your powers for your benefits.
- You will lack compassion and empathy.
- You may be overconfident and take things very lightly.

What happens when this chakra is OPEN or BALANCED?

- You will have a harmonious relationship with your surrounding and be more assertive in nature.
- You have clarity in what to do in your life. Your purpose, your goals will have a meaning defined.
- You will have high self-esteem, confidence and wisdom vibrating in you. You will feel powerful and be action oriented in your life which will help you achieve your purpose and goals.

How to balance or energize this chakra?

- Go out more in the Sun. Sun is the source of vitality and since this chakra represents element fire, getting energy directly from the sun helps you balance this energy. Early morning is preferable.
- Get to know yourself more in depth by asking questions to yourself. By asking many questions such as what are your strengths, talents, skills, weaknesses, what makes you happy, what activities stirs energy and enthusiasm inside you, and many more such questions will help you find your true sense, purpose and gain personal power.
- Personal affirmations will help you energize this chakra. "I am powerful and confident," "I am strong and courageous," "I embrace my strength," "I love the person I am," "I stand up for myself," "I am responsible for my

life," "I am worthy of love and kindness."

- Also eliminating your limiting self-beliefs (Step 2) help you energize this chakra.
- Eating foods which are yellow in color such as pineapple, bananas, Corn, Yellow dal, yellow capsicums, etc. helps you balance this chakra energy.
- Listen more to your gut feelings, try new things, practice public speaking.
- Best Yoga asanas to energize this chakra are Navasana (Boat Pose), Dhanurasana, Ardha Matsyendrasana, leg raising exercises.

The best tool to energize this Chakra – Meditation

You can close your eyes and start focusing on this Manipura chakra point for several minutes.

4th Chakra - *ANAHATA CHAKRA (HEART CHAKRA)*

This chakra is located exactly at center of your heart and the color it vibrates is **GREEN**

Symbol: Twelve petals positioned outside circle and a six-pointed star inside the circle and sound frequency is "YAM"

Characteristics of ANAHATA Chakra (Heart Chakra)

The main component of this chakra is LOVE and COMPASSION. This chakra is the bridge between material (earthly) and spiritual aspirations. This chakra is the integration point for lower 3 chakras and upper 3 chakras. This chakra empowers you with unconditional love for others and helps build strong relationships. This chakra represents Air element.

The Anahata chakra is all about connecting and relating. The emphasis here is on love, giving and receiving, and how open we are in relationships. Love is the energy that helps transfigure emotions and experiences. It's an essential element in any relationship, whether it is with others or oneself.

Love experienced through the fourth chakra is not just about romance, but about going beyond the limitations of the ego and personal preoccupations to open more fully to compassion and acceptance of all that is, as it is.

Your Soul also resides at the center of your heart and since this also coincides with the location of your Anahata chakra, the energy at this point is significant for body, mind, and soul energy synchronization.

Parts of the body associated with this chakra are the heart, lungs, respiratory system, thymus gland, hands, and arms.

What happens when this chakra is BLOCKED or IMBALANCED?

- You will not have the ability to love and accept other people and self. Due to this, you will have relationship issues.
- Lack of compassion: Hard-hearted, Cold or Lazy
- Heart and Respiratory ailments such as asthma. The weak immune system, upper back pain.
- Hand and arm related problems such as numbness, carpal tunnel, etc.
- Difficulty in forgiving others, holding on guilt for a long

time
- Most of the time you may feel lonely and feel no one cares for you.

What happens when this chakra is *OVERACTIVE?*

- Saying yes to everything and everyone, even when it does not benefit you
- You will lose your personal boundaries and start to make unhealthy choices, all in the name of love.
- You will start neglecting yourself and start giving more importance to others
- You will depend on others too much and lose your sense of identity.
- You may have heart palpitations, high blood pressure, and lung issues

What happens when this chakra is *OPEN* or *BALANCED?*

- You love and accept yourself and others readily.
- You take responsibility for your life and actions.
- You are a compassionate, joyful, peaceful and happy soul.
- You are able to forgive and trust others easily.
- You will have healthy and meaningful relationships
- You will have a healthy heart and lungs.

How to balance or energize this chakra?

- Due to past trauma, unresolved conflicts, circumstances and holding onto limiting beliefs may have caused blockages in this energy point. So, eliminating your limiting beliefs is a sure way to balance and energize this chakra (Step 2)
- Start loving yourself and others more. Radiate love from the bottom of your heart to your surroundings. Start seeing good things in others and appreciate them.
- Practice gratitude. This is the ultimate way to energize this energy point. Be thankful for the universe or God for all the things that happened or happening in all areas of your

life.
- Practice deep breathing exercises such as Pranayama and other yoga asanas
- Play with kids.

The best tool - Meditation

You can close your eyes and start focusing on this Anahata chakra point for several minutes.

5th Chakra - VISHUDDHI CHAKRA (THROAT CHAKRA)

This chakra is located exactly at center of your throat and the color it vibrates is **_BLUE_**

Symbol: 16 petals positioned outside circle and an inverted triangle inside the circle and inside the triangle a smaller circle with a moon crescent with a dot outside the triangle and sound frequency is "HAM"

Characteristics of VISHUDDHI Chakra (THROAT Chakra)

Vishuddhi chakra energy is based on the element Ether (Akasha). The main characteristic of this chakra is communication, expression, and creativity. The last 3 chakras including this Vishuddhi chakra is spiritual in nature and helps you to move to your higher consciousness.

This Chakra allows you to express yourself to the outer world, giving voice to the self, and enabling creative energies, ideas, visions, and dreams to flow and manifest. This chakra also oversees your openness to interaction and communication with others & with non-physical dimensions.

Speaking with a balanced throat chakra will enlighten and inspire those around you. This chakra helps you to be independent and have a firm grip over your thinking process. This energy enables you to express yourself openly and honestly in any situation with confidence.

This chakra enables you to connect with the etheric realm, the subtler realms of spirit and intuitive abilities. This chakra has a natural connection with the Swadhisthana chakra (sacral chakra), the center of emotions and creativity as well.

Because of its location, it's often seen as the "bottleneck" of the movement of energy in the body. It sits just before the upper chakras of the head. Balancing the energy of this Chakra can significantly help you align your vision with reality and release pressure that may affect the heart chakra that is located just below.

Parts of the body associated with this chakra are throat, thyroid gland, neck, mouth, tongue.

What happens when this chakra is BLOCKED or IMBALANCED?

-   You may have feelings of insecurity, timidity, and

119

introversion.

- You will have the inability to express and communicate clearly to the outside world and to yourself also.
- You will be closed minded, have behavioral problems, will lack clarity
- You will have chronic throat issues and dental problems.
- You will have shyness and do not open up with others and lack social interaction.
- You will have a problem connecting to higher powers.

What happens when this chakra is OVERACTIVE?

- Physical problems such as earaches, neck pain, and laryngitis occur.
- Dishonesty, excessive unwanted talking (You must have come across people who never stop speaking and eat your head), speaking rudely, arrogance.

What happens when this chakra is OPEN or BALANCED?

- You will be honest, truthful and firm in your communications with others as well as yourself.
- You will have clarity in what you communicate verbally as well as non-verbally.
- You will be highly active socially.
- You will express yourself with confidence, you will be a man of authenticity.
- Able to connect with higher realms of energy.

How to balance or energize this chakra?

- Drink more water regularly, this will help throat chakra balance the energy flow.
- Talk openly with family and friends, the more you openly talk with your feelings out, the movement of energy flows flexibly in this region and hence energizing the chakra.
- Speak the truth. Start journaling your daily activities. Be kind and spread more love to others.
- Stop judging yourself and others.

- Be in a clean environment with fresh air such as nature, rivers, oceans, etc.
- Vocalizing, singing, chanting prayers will balance and energize this chakra.
- Eating foods that are blue in color such as blueberries, raisins, etc. Having foods that soothe your throat is beneficial.
- Yoga asanas such as Halasana, Sarvangasana, tiger breathing, Matsyasana will help balance and energize this chakra.

The best tool - Meditation

You can close your eyes and start focusing on this Vishuddhi chakra point for several minutes.

6th Chakra - *AJNA CHAKRA (THIRD EYE CHAKRA)*

This chakra is located exactly between your eyebrows and the color it vibrates is ***INDIGO***

Symbol: 2 petals positioned outside circle and an inverted triangle inside the circle and sound frequency is "*OM*"

Characteristics of AJNA Chakra (THIRD EYE Chakra)

Ajna chakra energy helps you see the strengths beyond the physical world and connects you to higher powers of wisdom and consciousness. This chakra enables you to empower your intuition abilities, build a perception of subtle dimensions and movements of energy.

This chakra helps you build your Extra Sensory Perception. This chakra is an embodiment of all elements and senses.

This energy is useful to improve your memory, visualization capabilities, and all your 5 senses. It is also responsible for your higher awareness and spiritual development.

Parts of the body associated with this chakra are Brain, eyes, nose, sinus, nervous system, pineal gland, and pituitary glands.

This energy is also the seat of higher intellect and motivates inspiration and creativity.

What happens when this chakra is BLOCKED or IMBALANCED?

- You will have the inability to learn and receive guidance from others.
- You may suffer from depression or anxiety.
- You will feel stuck in your daily activities without being able to look beyond your problems and set a guiding vision for yourself.
- You will not be able to establish a vision for yourself and realize it.
- You will reject all the spiritual things in life and beyond
- You will lack clarity in thinking.
- Physically you will have headaches, migraine, sinusitis, poor vision, etc.
- You will ultimately lose connection with higher powers and beyond. You may be a disbeliever in GOD.

What happens when this chakra is *OVERACTIVE?*

- You may feel overwhelmed and engrossed in mental activities and delusions.
- You may have hallucinations and feel overstressed
- Severe headaches occurring frequently and may feel mentally fogged.
- Your thoughts keep wandering rapidly than usual and hence lack focus and concentration at a higher level.
- Inconsistent with your decisions and keep changing your choices every now and then. Kind of disbelief in yourself.

What happens when this chakra is *OPEN* or *BALANCED?*

- You will be tuned to higher awareness and consciousness. Will have tremendous clarity in your thinking and decisions.
- Your Spiritual faculties will be awakened and will start progressing to higher levels.
- You will start using your intuition abilities to your fullest and will have higher levels of knowledge and wisdom.
- You will go deep within yourself in silence smoothly.

How to balance or energize this chakra?

- If you feel this energy is blocked in you, you can go in silence and start observing yourself every day. Avoid distractions in your environment.
- If you feel like you are depressed or feeling low, it's best to be with people who can motivate, inspire and encourage you. Change your environment to more jovial and surround yourself with love and nature.
- Allow the creativity to flow in you.
- Chanting some prayers or mantra will balance the energy and energize this chakra.
- If you have overactive Agna chakra, then grounding yourself with your Mooladhara chakra with earth energy balances your Ajna chakra.
- Yoga asanas such as Uttanasana (Standing forward bend),

Sirsasana, Makarasana, Balasana and most important Nadi shuddhi Pranayama will energize and balance this Ajna chakra.

The best tool – Meditation

You can close your eyes and start focusing on this Agna chakra point for several minutes.

7th Chakra - *SAHASRARA CHAKRA (CROWN CHAKRA)*

This chakra is located slightly above your head and the color it vibrates is **_VIOLET_**

Symbol: 1000 petals positioned outside the circle and sound frequency is "_OM_"

Characteristics of SAHASRARA Chakra (CROWN Chakra)

This chakra can be described as a gateway to cosmic self or divine self. This energy helps you become one with consciousness. This is the energy center of spiritualism and enlightenment. Sahasrara chakra is beyond worldly elements and senses.

This chakra characterizes higher awareness, wisdom, and vision which is beyond your physical dimension. This Chakra enables connection with the formless, the limitless and integration with your Highest Self.

This chakra also governs your subconscious mind along with your conscious mind at the higher level and link you with divine energy and blends the physical and non-physical realms. You will experience Ecstasy and Bliss.

This Chakra influences your Brain, nervous system and emotions as well.

What happens when this chakra is BLOCKED or IMBALANCED?

- You will feel disconnected spiritually and also with higher energies and realms.
- You will lack clarity and will have no direction in your life.
- You will lack the ability to connect with others.
- You may feel lonely and depressed.
- Neurological disorders and other psychological problems.
- You may feel depressed, have mental fogginess and psychological problems.
- You may lack empathy.
- You are completely confused and clueless.
- You may have seizures
- You may be very sensitive to light.

What happens when this chakra is OPEN or BALANCED?

- You will have tremendous trust in yourself and your inner guidance.
- You will be more receptive to draw spiritual energies from higher powers.
- You will be able to live in your personal presence and enjoy life to the fullest.
- You will be an inspiration to others and a guiding light to many individuals and groups.

How to balance or energize this chakra?

- Restoring balance to this Sahasrara chakra is very important to maintaining a healthy balance within your chakra system overall.
- To balance or energize this chakra, first, you must take care of all the other 6 chakras especially your Mooladhara chakra so that you remain grounded.
- Tune into nature and spend more time.
- Visualization techniques help you activate this energy.
- Yoga asanas such as Surya Namaskar, Garudasana, Padmasana, Sirsasana and pranayama will help you balance and energize this chakra.

The best tool – Meditation

You can close your eyes and start focusing on this Sahasrara chakra point for several minutes.

Now that you are aware of energies and chakras and its implications, you can analyze your own life and find out where your energies are blocked and where it is balanced. As you have learned in Step 1 the importance of personal presence, in this step 4 it is imperative to be aware of your energies. You need to practice consciously to be mindful of the energies and get a feel of it. As you practice this awareness of energy consciously every day, you begin to feel more sensitive to energies inside you and outside you.

All the chakras are well connected and help each other to balance the energies. Deficiency of energy in any one chakra can affect different chakra energies. How these chakra energies vibrate determine the health of your Aura. As you know Aura is generated from the Chakras. The bigger the aura you have, the more you will attract prosperity and shine brighter in all areas of your life.

If there is an imbalance in your energies, there are many healing methods and techniques that you can adapt to recharge your energies and balance them. But the best I find is "MEDITATION." Yes, meditation can heal your energy imbalances and help you have a life to the fullest.

Before ending this chapter, I would like to provide you 1 simple technique to energize your energies

1 Simple Technique to Energize yourself

At night, before going to bed every day, just sit straight and pray to the **Universal divine** to send golden rays of light through your Sahasrara chakra and fill your entire body with golden rays of light and energize all my chakras and my physical body. With this intention and thought go to sleep.

I do this technique every day, and this was taught to me by my uncle **Dr. Y.K Madhav Rao**, and this has been very beneficial to me.

Thoughts and intentions have the ultimate power to manifest anything in your life. You just need to ask for it, and you will be given.

Step 5 - EVOLVE TO YOUR HIGHER SELF

5 - Step Model To Reach Your Higher Consciousness

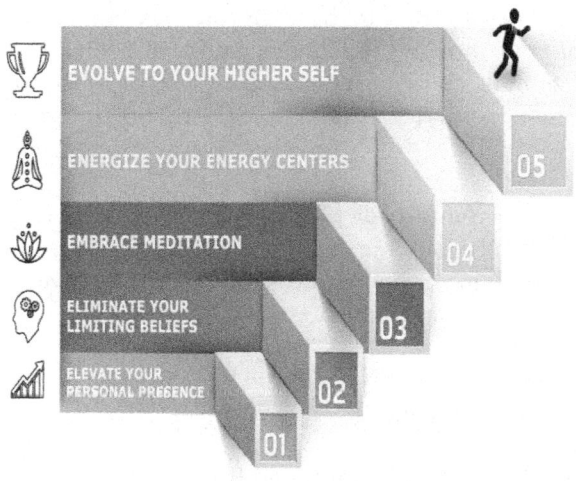

"When you are evolving to your higher self, the road seems lonely. But you are simply shedding energies that no longer match the frequency of your destiny."

To evolve to your higher self means raising your quality of life to the highest level, it also means living in a higher vibrational energy state. And for this to happen you need to increase the vibrations of your thoughts, intentions, and actions in your day to day life with at most consciousness. And to raise the quality of your thoughts, intentions and actions it is essential to Synergize your Soul, Mind, and Body.

When you move into your Higher Self with Higher Conscious levels with high energy and maintain this energy levels, you will be able to manifest abundance in all areas of your life and live your life with passion, love, joy, and happiness.

In Step 5, EVOLVE to your HIGHER SELF, you will learn how to evolve to your higher self in 3 parts, and they are

1. Synergize your Soul, Mind, and Body.
2. Finding your true identity (Your Purpose, Mission & Vision)
3. Manifest abundance in all areas of your life (Connecting to and Trusting Universal Energies). In short, I call it **"ABUNDANCE FLOW."**

CHAPTER 7:

POWER OF SYNERGIZING SOUL, MIND AND BODY

Synergize Soul, Mind, Body ——▶Raise your quality of thoughts, intentions & actions ——▶ Living in your higher vibrational energy frequency ——▶ Evolve to your Higher Self.

Synergize Soul, Mind, Body ⟹ **Evolve to your Higher Self**

So, let's first understand what do I mean by Synergizing your Soul, Mind, and Body. Synergizing is aligning the energy vibrations of your body, mind, and soul. In simple terms, it is you being congruent both inside (Soul & Mind) and outside (Physical Body) of yourself.

To synergize these 3 entities, you must take utmost care and nourish these 3 entities Soul, Mind and Body. All 3 are interlinked, and you cannot ignore anyone. According to research, almost 90% of people in this world ignore either one of them or all of them and hence have imbalance in their lives and cannot operate at their highest energy levels and consciousness and surrender themselves to a mediocre life where "Life happens to you," and people are content with what's happening to their survival. People think nothing can be done about it and say this is the way life is and blame it on luck. People believe in this way because they lack knowledge, wisdom, experiences, better environment and most important people are not ready to receive knowledge and energies.

Before learning how to nourish your Soul, Mind and Body let's see what these 3 entities are.

Every human being on this planet earth are wonderful Soul beings. Each of these souls has taken the physical body as it's vehicle. The soul is nothing but a particle of light from the ocean of light, which is the source of all creations. So, we can say we are light beings. Soul has awareness, individuality, and free will.

The mind is an unseen powerful entity every human has. Mind is like the bridge between your physical body and Soul. Soul carries thoughts that originate from our intellect to our physical brain. The mind is a channel through which we experience all the things in the physical world. Whenever our soul desires certain things to do, this desire is communicated through mind to our physical brain, and our physical brain can convert this desire into physical action through our complex nervous system. Through our 5 physical senses, we create and have the experiences and pass on these experiences back to our soul through Mind.

The mind can also be called as awareness, and it has 4 levels of consciousness. They are

- Conscious Mind
- Subconscious Mind
- Unconscious Mind
- Super Conscious Mind

Conscious Mind is nothing but, you are entirely aware of what's happening around you such as you are thoroughly consciously reading this book.

Subconscious Mind is part wakefulness and part sleep. This subconscious mind is like a master which gives commands to your conscious mind to carry out actions, and your conscious mind must follow it. You can access your subconscious mind when you are between awakened and sleep state. That is when you are about to go to sleep or when you just got up from sleep.

Unconscious Mind is a state of deep sleep when your entire system is relaxing. You will not know what is happening around you when you are in this state. You do not have any experiences.

Super Conscious Mind is a state in which you are in total silence and total awareness but not in sleep. This state can be reached only through meditation. In this state of mind, you can connect to universal energies and experience the unknown.

The 3rd entity is our physical body which is the most complex living mechanism on planet earth. This physical body is only a vehicle for the soul to have experiences on this planet.

Soul, Mind, and body are energies vibrating at different frequencies.

As we saw what is Soul, Mind, and Body, let's understand why these 3 entities need to be synergized?

Why do we need to synergize Soul, Mind, and Body?

The answer to this question is very simple and straightforward.

"To have absolute CLARITY in LIFE"

Without clarity in life, you know what will happen. To have absolute clarity in life, it is crucial to synergize your soul, mind, and body.

How to synergize Soul, Mind, and Body?

We spend so much time learning many subjects such as history, mathematics, science, language, arts and many more subjects in school. We learn how to ride a bike, cook, perform job tasks and how to advance in our careers and discover many more things. And yet, we neglect to learn the one thing that affects every single aspect of our lives. It's the communication between our body, mind, and soul.

There is a communication loop between these three aspects of ourselves. When these three parts of you are incongruent, your life will feel chaotic, and you will find it difficult to move forward and manifest your dreams. If you want to take charge of the direction of your life, you need to learn how to get them into vibrational alignment.

Everything in your current environment is a vibrational match to your own vibrational frequency. You are always broadcasting a vibration out into the universe, and therefore, you attract only that which is of the same vibrational quality. Everything you experience is a reflection of your vibrational state.

So, look around. Do you like what you have created...your finances, your relationships, your health, etc.? It is all a reflection of what is going on in your vibration. If you are completely and utterly happy with every part of your life, then you are in alignment...pat yourself on your back!

But, if you are like 99% of the population, there is something in some area of your life that you can't seem to manifest. Maybe it is the loving relationship, or the income you are generating, or new entrepreneurial venture. Whatever it is, you want it, but you don't have it. If what you want does not match what is showing up in your experience, then you are NOT in alignment with your Soul, Mind, and Body.

Let's say suppose you had an idea or a desire, and you felt inspired at that moment and want to fulfill this desire. Soon after this initial inspiration and excitement, you start to have thoughts of fear whether you will be able to accomplish this idea or desire. These resistant thoughts will give you all the reasons why you can't fulfill your wishes.

So, the idea of a new business, new venture, new action or new relationship would inevitably be followed by your fears mainly about money, survival and many other factors. Your mind is out of vibrational alignment with your soul. Your Soul is vibrationally aligned with your desire, but your thoughts at the level of consciousness, are not aligned, and due to this your body also does not get aligned, and you are- not able to take action.

Because of these fear-based thoughts, most of the people (99% of the population) stop imagining / dreaming / believing their desires and give up thinking about it.

Now here is a **secret** that you can apply to push your desire further to your Mind and then to your body and take massive actions in fulfilling your desires.

Whenever you have resistant thoughts, just remind yourself and say this to yourself.

"Hey, I wouldn't be able to have this idea or desire if it wasn't attainable and aligned with my higher self and purpose."

When you remind and say this to yourself, your belief in your idea or desire strengthens. The thoughts or the desires that come to you have a specific purpose in your life, and hence they come to you, but most of them you do not hold on to it and give up easily without understanding the reason or purpose of the ideas or desires popping up in your life.

Once you understand when specific ideas or desires keep coming up every now and then, you should immediately realize that there is some purpose for them to show up in you. Maybe this idea or desire is an indication for me to evolve to my higher self, move to my next higher version. When you remind yourself of such enhancing thoughts of higher vibration, it enables you to continue to allow yourself to imagine your idea or desire.

As you imagine it, you would attract even more powerful thoughts that are in vibrational alignment with that desire. Then, you would begin to feel something. The inspiration has come from your soul, then into your mind, and then penetrating the dimension of your body. The doorway between your mind and your body is EMOTION.

Your emotional body is like a membrane between your physical body and your mental body. Emotions are what translate your thoughts into physical sensation at the level of the body.

For example, take a minute, and remember an event in your life. An event like the death of a loved one, or maybe a happy event, like the birth of your child. Let yourself remember it, just for a moment.

You could feel the emotions, couldn't you? Did the mere thought of that event, bring back the rush of emotion that you had at that time? Where did you feel that emotion? You thought about it partially in your mind, and partly in your physical body, right? Maybe you felt it in the pit of your stomach or felt tears come off your eyes. At the same time, your first memory would have been followed by thoughts related to and matching the vibration of that event, compounding the sadness, or fear, or happiness.

Your thoughts inspire emotions which cause a reaction in your physical body. So, now you can see the connection between your body, mind, and soul, right?

Hence, it is essential to scale up your vibrations at Mind and body level. Because most of the desires or ideas originate from your soul. To fulfill the desires of your soul, action needs to be taken at a physical level with the help of your mind power. When the vibrations at your mind and physical level are raised and enhanced it becomes easier to accomplish your dreams and desires.

Understanding this reality changed my perspective about life and how it works. When I realized this concept of synergizing soul, mind, and body, I started observing successful people and researched and studied the habits and values of these successful people. What do they do to raise their energy vibrations at mind and body level? I found so many common things that these people have in them.

Below are the ways to raise your vibrations at your Mind and Body level so that you can synergize your Soul, Mind, and Body:

Nourish your Physical Health

1. For your body to function optimally, your food habits are the most important. Your body requires the right nutrition. Are you giving right and enough nutrients to your body **every day?**

Are you conscious about eating healthy food?
Are you chewing your food enough before swallowing?
Are you eating your food slowly?

"I believe your fitness and health is more dependent on food (75%) you eat than the exercises (25%) you do."

Eating natural and seasoned foods are always better to get the highest energy to your body. And more important to get the best result from a healthy diet is to set an intention before eating the food in your mind: **"Let me get the best energies and vibrations from this food. Thank You"**

2. Keeping yourself physically active by doing regular exercises of your choice. Stretching your muscles every now and then every day is the key to keep stress far away. Make a habit of doing specific exercise every day both morning and evening for at least 15 mins. This advice may seem very simple and familiar. But how many of them really do it daily?

Only when you do it consistently, you can start feeling the vibrations of your body raising to higher levels.

Again, it is necessary to do your stretches and exercises consciously to feel those vibrations raising.

To get the best energies and raise your physical energy

vibrations set an intention before doing your exercises in your mind: **"Let me get best energies and vibrations from these exercises. Thank You"**

3. Manage your Physical stress

    You need to provide adequate rest to your body to re-energize and heal time to time. You need to be conscious enough to know when to give your physical body the rest it needs. Always see to it you have good and quality sleep every day.

4. Avoid sitting for more extended periods and have correct postures.

5. Regularly detoxify yourself. You need to detoxify your internal systems as well as your outer body. Internal detoxification can be done in many ways under proper guidance. Outer detoxification can also be done in many ways. Some of the ideas are to have body massages that can rejuvenate, and you can have a salt water bath.

Nourish your Mind

1. Proper and Regulated Breathing

Energy vibrations at your Mind level can be raised to its higher levels by proper and conscious breathing. Yes! Proper regulated breathing can raise vibrations at your mind level.

You can practice "Pranayama" or any other breathing techniques you know. By consistently practicing these breathing techniques your awareness about your energy levels also increases and you can start feeling the vibrations increasing at your mind level.

2. Remove unnecessary worries from your Mind.

Most of the time, people start worrying about the things that are never going to happen in the future. Most of the time the little voice in your head keeps scaring you and always puts you in doubt about your capabilities causing unnecessary worries. These worries lower your vibrational energy at the mind level and cause blockages.

You need to realize consciously that your little voice in your head is taking charge of you and stop that voice in your head by replacing it with positive and inspiring affirmations every day such as **"I am capable of solving any challenges thrown at my life easily"**.

There are so many mind power strategies that people learn in my signature program
"Absolute Mind Champion - Unlock your Energies." The above is one among them- "Affirmations."

3. Manage your emotional stress

You have to manage your emotional stress by just being aware of your emotions. Only by being aware of your feelings, when any situation arises that can imbalance your senses and make you react at that moment, you can control your emotions by knowing consciously and respond to the situation rather than reacting to it.

4. Overcoming your fears and limiting beliefs

Fears and limiting beliefs cause most of the damages in your life without you realizing it. Hence most of the people are stuck in their lives and living a mediocre life. This is the main reason why your energy vibrations are lower at your mind as well as physical level.

To overcome this, you can follow "Step 2 - Eliminate your limiting beliefs" in this book.

5. Self-Observation

Observing your thoughts and intentions consciously. Spend time alone every day for a few mins and relax. Do not overthink as this is not good for your mind. Simplicity is the best way.

Energize your Environment

Have a clutter-free home and work environment

If you want to focus on best of your abilities, have more clarity, be super productive and enhance the energy vibrations around you, then you need to clear clutter from your home and work environment. It is crucial to remove clutter every now and then from your surroundings. This clutter blocks your energies and creates low vibrations, which in turn affects your mind and body level vibrations to come down.

Keeping all your rooms in the house neat and tidy is a must. Remove all unwanted things that you don't use from your home and workplace. Segregate all the stuff into 3 categories.

The first category - All the things that you want to give away to somebody who is in need.
The second category - All the things that you want to throw away.
The third category - All the things you need to keep for yourself.

Now keep all the things you need in an organized way so that your place looks neat and beautiful. As time goes, unwanted items get piled up. So, this task of decluttering needs to be done frequently at your home and also at your workplace.

To enhance the energies further, you can also decorate your home with natural flowers, good fragrances and even by having good inspiring sounds of music played and by putting good scenic pictures on the walls.

By enhancing the vibrations of your environment helps you synergize your 3 entities.

Be with nature more often.

Being with nature such as open spaces, trees, playgrounds, parks, mountains, rivers, oceans, waterfalls, forests, etc. helps you to raise your vibrations to higher levels. When you are in these places consciously become aware of the things around you with all your 5 senses.

Be Happy

Learn to be happy from within. When you are happy, and then when you perform your actions, results are more guaranteed. Happiness has very high energy vibration frequency. So being in this happy state naturally raises your vibrational frequency at all levels. Make a habit to be in this happy state in autopilot mode.

Be in your Personal presence.

Being in the present and your universal presence is the key to move to your higher self. Step 1 - Elevating your personal presence teaches you how to be in your personal presence. Kindly refer to chapter 2 again.

Socialize with high energy positive people

"You become the average of 5 people with whom you spend your time the most."

Your circle of friends and people matter the most. If you want to be super active, energetic, enthusiastic, massive action taker and successful, you need to spend time only with such kind of people who have these qualities that you want to have.

Surrender your EGO

Let go off all those small little things and unnecessary things that do not add any value to your life. Your life is short to carry the unwanted burden all along the journey. Let go off your ego and start radiating love to yourself and people around you.

Laugh more and Travel more

Experience the joy with every laugh. Laugh more with others but not on others. Share your joy and happiness.

Traveling to different places gives you different perspectives about yourself, about the world, about the people. You will have a fantastic life learnings and experiences when you travel, and this will definitely raise your level of vibrations and help you synergize.

"Your Soul is here to experience the beauty of life on earth. So, have amazing life experiences."

CHAPTER 8:

POWER OF FINDING YOUR IDENTITY: YOUR MISSION AND VISION

You just saw how synergizing your soul, mind, and body helps you to evolve to your Higher Self.

"There is no greater gift you can give or receive than to honor your calling. It's why you were born. And how you become most truly alive." —Oprah Winfrey

To evolve to your Higher self, it is also essential that you must know your Purpose of Life. That is, you should know what is your personal life Mission statement is.

Knowing your purpose of life and your Mission statement gives you the direction in which you need to take your life ahead with focus, passion, and commitment.

To make sure you understand the difference between your Purpose of life and your mission statement of life. Here it is:

Mission: What you want to do?
Purpose: Why you want to do it?
Vision: Vision is a vehicle to accomplish your Mission so that you fulfill your purpose. (Where do you want to see yourself in future say 5-15 years)

For example, let us consider my mission and my purpose and my vision to better understand what these 3 are:

My Mission (What do I want to do in my life):

"Inspire, Teach and Train Human beings to reach their Higher conscious levels so that they live their life with Passion, Joy, Happiness, and Love."

My Purpose (Why I want to do what I want to do)

I want to accomplish my Mission because (**My BIG WHY?**):

I have suffered a lot living a mediocre life in an autopilot mode for many years and seen and seeing many people still living an mediocre life and suffering a lot. And the main reason that I find people live a mediocre life is because of lower levels of consciousness and lower vibrations of energy. I firmly believe that the purpose of life is to express your higher self with passion, joy, happiness, and love. You need to move from life of mediocrity to a life of Excellence with higher consciousness. When this happens, life is a pure joy and you have amazing experiences.

I want every human being on this planet earth to have such kind of life and also live *MY LIFE* with **Passion, Joy, Happiness, and Love**

Hence my mission is to "Inspire, Teach and Train Human beings to reach their Higher conscious levels so that people live their life with Passion, Joy, Happiness, and Love."

My Vision (Where do I see myself in coming 3,5,10,15 years)

146

You need to have the vision to accomplish your Mission. You need to decide where do you want to be in the next 3 years, 5 years, 10 years and 15 years which is in alignment with your Mission.

Here is my vision which is in alignment with my Mission

1. To be one of the world's best trainer and sought out speaker on Higher Consciousness, Mind Power and Energies.

2. Inspire and train 10 lakh (1 million) people in the next 5 years.

3. Grow my training company globally in 100 countries and empower people in the area of self-development and consciousness in the next 10 years.

4. Collaborate with top leaders in the world in the self-development industry in the next 3 years.

5. Become the world's bestselling author for all my books so that my message reaches out and inspires to as many people in the world.

6. Have my own charitable trust to provide quality education to the poor.

7. Travel the world and have amazing life experiences and have beautiful relationships with the people around me.

So, you get the clear distinction between your Mission, your purpose and your Vision. At times people combine your purpose and Mission together as your (BIG WHY?). Here I am keeping these separate so that you have a clear distinction.

Why do you need to have your personal Mission and Vision?

1. Knowing your personal mission, purpose and vision gives you a proper direction in life and can live a meaningful life which provides you with real joy.

2. Knowing your purpose gives you clarity and simplifies your decision-making process. It helps you have clear goals, clear plans and clear actions which are in complete alignment.

3. It helps you decide what is essential and what is unimportant. Most of the people today are caught up doing entirely unimportant things which have no meaning and value in their lives. Their time and energy are exhausted in doing these trivial things.

4. It helps you have tremendous focus and constant drive in your life, which helps you build your character and values.

5. When you are in the journey of fulfilling your purpose, the journey itself is so pleasant, memorable and exciting that every day, every hour you spend in this journey gives you a sense of satisfaction from within because you are delighted pursuing this incredible journey.

6. You are so passionate that time flies by and you do not feel tired in spite of working for long hours.

7. When you have a purpose, mission, and vision in your life, you automatically live more consciously and attract all the required divine universal energies that help you to accomplish and fulfill your goals, mission, and purpose.

I firmly believe that once you have your purpose, mission, and vision, you need not worry about how you can achieve them. "How part" is taken care by itself because you are so deeply involved into it that your thoughts, intentions, focus, time and energy are entirely aligned and believe me the universe is behind you as a wall to make it happen in reality.

Currently, I am in my journey of fulfilling my purpose and accomplishing my mission. Initially, when this journey started I had doubts on how will I do it, but believe me, I get automatically guided by the universe as to what my next step should be, what my next goal should be, what my next action should be. I go with the flow as the universe guides me through my intuition and I have complete faith in it. When I mean full faith, it's absolute faith. I do not have even a single iota of doubt on universal guidance.

With this faith, you just need to take MASSIVE ACTIONS that is required to make it happen in reality whenever you get guidance from the universe.

This guidance can be in many forms, you need to be more conscious in identifying it. You can receive guidance through some new opportunities, it can be new people or people you already know. Guidance can come in the form of situations, sudden creative ideas flashing out from nowhere. Some of these ideas can flash only for a second and then may disappear forever. In such circumstances, it is essential to make a note of these flashy ideas somewhere so that later you can analyze it and deep dive deep into it. Guidance's can also be in the form of books, magazines, articles, movies, songs, videos, etc. Sometimes you get guidance in your dreams too.

For me, most of my guidance comes when I am meditating. So, meditation has been profoundly impactful in my life. **Embrace Meditation (Step 3)** so that you too can have such a profound positive impact in your life.

You may ask me a question; how will I know if this is the right guidance I need to follow?

90% of your thoughts are made of gut feeling and intuition. The remaining 10% is logic.

Your initial feeling when you have a specific thought or an intention or an idea gives you sound vibrations of positivity and makes you feel good. Most people do not identify this initial feeling because they have not elevated their personal presence and are not much conscious enough and miss the opportunity to recognize guidance. Hence it is essential to elevate your own existence (Step 1).

If you can identify this initial feeling and intuition, then you can apply your logic along with this and make a decision whether you need to take a step forward. Most of the time this initial thought would be the right one to follow. Again, you need to keep practicing this to master it.

You now learned why it is so important to have your Mission and Purpose and need not to worry about the how part because universal energies and forces are there to make it happen.

Now let's see what questions you need to ask yourself to find what your Mission and purpose is in life?

To do this exercise, I highly recommend you to be in a good state of mind, relaxed, energetic and not in the empty stomach. I am telling these things precisely because you are not going to do some school homework, you will be doing your **Life homework**, and lots of thinking is required, and your brain consumes most of the energy.

Some more Instructions

- Take out a few sheets of paper and a pen.
- Find a place where you will not be interrupted. Turn off your cell phone.
- Write down the answers to each of the questions. Write the first thing that pops into your head. Write without editing. Use point form. It's important to write out your answers rather than just think about them.
- Write quickly. Give yourself less than 60 seconds for a question. Preferably less than 30 seconds.
- Be honest. Nobody will read it. Writing without editing is essential.
- Enjoy the moment and smile as you write.

Questions to find out your purpose and Mission

1. What were your dreams and desires in the past when you were a child?

2. What are your current dreams and desires?

3. What makes you Smile (Activities, people, events, hobbies, projects, etc.)?

4. What makes you feel great about yourself?

5. What activities make you lose track of time?

6. What are your strengths?

7. What are you good at?

8. What talents do other people recognize in you?

9. What do people typically ask you for help in?

10. If you had to teach something, what would you teach?

11. What would you regret not thoroughly doing, being or having in your life?

12. What gives you a sense of satisfaction and fulfillment?

13. What are your deepest core values?

Values represent what you stand for. They express your uniqueness and individuality. Values guide your behavior, and they help you in empowering yourself. When you honor your personal core values consistently, you experience a sense of fulfillment and joy.

My top core values that I live my life with are:
- High Energy
- Higher Consciousness
- Passion
- Love and Happiness
- Learning and Growing
- Taking right Massive action in-spite of having fear

Please select 3-5 words, and put in order most important to you:

Achievement	Intelligence
Adventure	Intimacy
Beauty	Joy
Being the best	Leadership
Challenge	Learning
Comfort	Love
Courage	Motivation
Creativity	Passion
Curiosity	Performance
Education	Personal growth
Empowerment	Play
Environment	Productivity
Family	Primary
Financial freedom	Relationship
Fitness	Reliability
Friendship	Respect
Giving I service	Security
Health	Spirituality
Honesty	Success
Independence	Time freedom
Inner peace	Variety
Integrity	

You can list any other values which are not present here.

14. What were some challenges, difficulties, and hardships you've overcome or are in the process of overcoming? How did you do it?

15. Given your talents, passions, and values. How could you use these resources to serve, help, contribute? (to people, beings, causes, organization, environment, planet, etc.)

Now that you have answered all the questions, you can observe that you have one or more common answers to most of these questions. Identify and mark them separately. With these common and repeating answers, you can figure out and analyze what you genuinely want to do in your life from the bottom of your heart and also why you want to do it? (Your BIG WHY?) knowing which is your purpose.

Creating your Personal Mission statement

"Writing or reviewing a mission statement changes you because it forces you to think through your priorities deeply, carefully, and to align your behavior with your beliefs."

~Stephen Covey

Let us see how to create your personal mission statement using an example of my mission statement.

"**Inspire, Teach and Train** *Human beings* **to reach their Higher conscious levels so that they live their life with Passion, Joy, Happiness and Love**."

The mission statement is divided into 3 parts.

Part 1 - What action you want to perform.?

Here I want to "**Inspire, teach and Train**"

Similarly, you can use some of the below action words in framing your Mission statement:

Educate, accomplish, empower, encourage, improve, help, give, guide, inspire, integrate, master, motivate, nurture, organize, produce, promote, travel, spread, share, satisfy, understand, teach, write, etc.

Part 2 - Whom do you want to help?

Here I want to help "**Human beings**"

Similarly, you can write who do you want to help? Some examples are People, creatures, organizations, causes, groups, environment, etc.

Part 3 - What value / benefit you want to create?

Value that I intend to create is "help people **to reach their Higher conscious levels so that they live their life with Passion, Joy, Happiness and Love**.

Similarly, you can write what value you want to create?

Your Purpose (Why?)

Now that you have framed your Mission statement, you can state your purpose as to why you want to do this in 1 or more sentences as I have stated my purpose at the beginning of this chapter.

To give you some more example of Mission, Purpose, values, and vision other than mine, let's take a look at Southwest Airlines company.

Southwest Airline Mission:

"The mission of Southwest Airlines is dedication to the highest quality of Customer Service delivered with a sense of warmth, friendliness, individual pride, and Company Spirit."

Here part 1 - What action they want to do?
"Dedicate themselves to provide highest quality service."

Part 2 - Whom do they want to help? - "Their Customers"

Part 3 - What value/benefit they are creating?
"Deliver service with a sense of warmth, friendliness, individual pride, and Company Spirit."

Southwest Airline Purpose:

"Connect People to what's important in their lives through friendly, reliable, and low-cost air travel."

Can you see their purpose: "They want to connect people to what's important in their lives." This airline is concerned about people's happiness, and hence they speak about **"Connecting"** people to **"What's important to their lives"** at **"low-cost air travel which is also reliable and friendly."**

How beautiful isn't it?

Southwest Airline Vision:

"To become the world's most loved, most flown, and most profitable airline."

Southwest Airline Values:

Live the Southwest Way:
Warrior Spirit
Servant's Heart
Fun-LUVing Attitude

Work the Southwest Way
Safety and Reliability
Friendly Customer Service and Low Costs

Some of the points to remember while creating your Mission (This I learned from my mentor during my training) are:

Putting these points directly as it is written in my notebook for your benefit.

- Everyone has a mission including you and me.
- Your Mission may not be fulfilled in this lifetime.

- Your Mission encompasses both your personal and business life.
- Your Mission is not your Job / Business (Your Job / Business can be part of your Mission but not your Mission).
- Your Mission is not your role (e.g., Father / Son / ...)
- Your Mission is based on serving others.
- Your Mission is based on Action.
- Your Mission does not have to be huge.
- Your Mission has nothing to do with Money (Money should be a byproduct/result of what value you contribute). The money will flow in abundance automatically when your focus is purely on creating tremendous amount and massive impact on others life.
- Your Mission is your Soul's work.
- Your Mission excites you and ignites a passion for or against something.
- Your Mission is something that you can control on your end.

Now that you are clear in creating your Mission, purpose, and values, it's time for you to write down your Vision.

As explained earlier Vision is nothing but where do you see yourself in the future to accomplish your mission and fulfill your purpose.

Vision is always backtracked. That is, you need to see yourself where you will be say in next 15 - 20 years. Then backtrack to 10 years from now, then backtrack to 5 years from now, 3 years, 1 year, 6 months, 1 month so on.

Some people think of the future in terms of generations. Such people belong to elite leaders group, and they are called Visionary persons.

Start creating your Vision statements and be bold enough to **THINK BIG**. As I said earlier do not worry about how to achieve them as Universe will take care of it. You just need to think really Big as to how you can contribute and create an impact.

10 Year Vision:
5 Year Vision:
3 Year Vision:
1 Year Vision:
6 months Vision:

Once you create your vision statements, write all your Mission, Purpose, Vision and values on a sheet of paper and stick these papers in your room, office so that these things are seen easily and keeps reinstating into your subconscious mind every day.

"Embracing Meditation will definitely help you find your Mission, purpose, vision, and values faster" - I am telling you all these based on my personal experiences.

Create your own identity by finding your mission, purpose, vision, and values so that you can evolve further into your Higher Self and live your life with higher consciousness and great energy.

CHAPTER 9:

ABUNDANCE FLOW: CONNECTING AND TRUSTING HIGHER UNIVERSAL POWERS

One of my strongest core belief is:

"Universe has everything in abundance to give for us, it's only that we need to ask for it and be open to receive it with both arms."

Earlier when I was living a mediocre life, with low vibrational frequencies, life just happened to me and was always in thoughts such as

"Today let there be no more challenges."
"Fear of not getting into any trouble."
"Spend time watching all movies, tv shows."
"It's OK to do tomorrow or later, let me relax now."
"No commitment and No self-accountability."
"Fear of taking any small risk."
"Why should I bother attitude."
"What is my gain by doing this?"

And many more such mediocre thoughts ran all through my

mind. Now, you tell me how in this world I could have attracted abundance in my life. When most of my dreams, intentions, and actions were of low vibrational energy, how could I have drawn abundance flow in my life and this was the main reason why I suffered for 8 long years.

I am grateful to universal divine and the universe that I could come out of this mediocre, unfulfilling, non-exciting, unhappy and boring life and able to live my life with passion, joy, happiness and more important living my life with ABUNDANCE in all areas of my life.

Now that you know what keeps you at the high vibrational frequency and how to be in high energy state:

This 5-step model in the book:

Step 1 - **Elevate** your Personal Presence
Step 2 - **Eliminate** your Limiting Beliefs
Step 3 - **Embrace** Meditation
Step 4 - **Energize** your Energy Centers
Step 5 - **Evolve** to your Higher Self

In this final part (Part 3) of final step to move to your Higher Conscious levels, it's all about connecting yourself to universal energies and trusting the universe to have abundance flow in all areas of your life. As I said Universe has everything to offer that you desire, you just need to evolve to your higher self by *Connecting* and *Trusting* the universe.

Connecting to Universe

This 5-step model itself helps you to connect to the higher universal powers and move you to your higher vibrational energy frequencies. Below are the ways to strengthen this connection, which is already established.

1) Have a feel-good factor throughout your day

To strengthen your connection with the universe, it's essential for you to know how do you feel in your entire day. Do you feel good most of your day? Do you feel low and stressed most of your day? Do you feel calm and peaceful inside no matter what's the situation is outside surrounding you?

When you elevate yourself and feel good, energetic and happy from inside out throughout the day automatically, you are pushing yourself to your higher selves. Never allow yourself to have a single dull moment in your life.

2) Deep awareness in all aspects of your life

When you have a sense of profound awareness in each of the actions you take, you are more present. You need to consider every minute details as necessary. Because these minute details are the ones which give you different perspectives in life.

3) Be Grounded

Grounding yourself to earth element is very crucial time to time. Grounding helps your Mooladhara chakra to strengthen and keeps your physical essence intact. Since you are part of this physical earth and you possess a physical body, it's crucial to take care of this physical body. It may so happen that sometimes you allow yourself to be drawn away from physical action in your life. Grounding helps you to take that physical action in your life which is required to fulfill your purpose and mission.

4) Focus more on Love and Compassion

Love and compassion are the energies of higher frequencies. When you radiate energy, which is of Love and kindness to others, naturally you will strengthen your connection with the universe.

5) Become a better version of yourself every day

In simple terms what I say is "You need to grow personally." To become a better version of yourself every day, you need to have **"2 most important qualities in you."**

"Commitment" - Do you have a 100% commitment to yourself and others every time? Your results in life will tell you how much committed you are. Just take a few minutes and self-reflect on yourself and your results.

"Self-Accountability" - Are you ready to take complete ownership and responsibility of your actions and results. It requires honesty, self-reflection and a clear identity and belief in what you are doing. When you have these, you can admit to any shortcomings and hold yourself accountable rather than making excuses or blaming external factors.

Trusting the Universe

Only when you completely trust the universe and be in a **state of Allowing**, Abundance flows into your life from all directions.

You can trust the universe in the below ways:

1) Trust your Intuition

Everybody has this power of using their intuition, but very few use it. Intuition helps you download all the required information, knowledge or wisdom that you need at that moment from the higher power or universe. You need to trust your intuition.

Usually, the very first thought / intention / idea that comes to your mind when you think about a certain thing or deciding is intuition-based thought / idea. Typically, such intuition-based thoughts or ideas last for very few seconds in your mind, and there is a high probability you may forget or do not remember it later. Keep working on using your intuition more often.

2) Be a Good Giver and an Excellent Receiver

"You can give only that which you have."

When you have something that you want to give it away to some needy, you feel very happy and fulfilled because you have just satisfied one of your 6 human needs **"CONTRIBUTION"** according to Tony Robbins.

But at the same time, you feel hesitated or shy or uncomfortable at the physical level or at thought level when someone is giving to you. You have some kind of perception or notion about yourself that I don't deserve this, and I should not be taking or receiving this. You are creating the block for yourself knowingly or unknowingly.

Keep telling yourself **"I am an excellent receiver."** Saying this affirmation helps you to become a natural and excellent receiver.

3) Ask help from the Universe through thoughts and intentions

Whenever you feel you need guidance or more clarity in any aspect of your life, ask help from the universe through your thoughts and intentions with complete trust. You will definitely get guidance through some or the other form. You just need to ask the universe with ***complete trust.***

4) Detach yourself from the outcome

This is where most of them go wrong completely. People do everything right till this point and get frustrated that results are not showing in their life. The main reason results are not showing up is because people are attached to the results, they are so desperate to make it happen at any cost. You have so many expectations from others and from yourself that you are not able to focus on your thoughts and intentions and finally make your mind a place of clutter.

Where there is no focus, energy does not converge at one point, energy spreads across, and there is no calm and peace. And due to this, you cannot radiate love. Calm, peace and love are the highest vibrational frequencies.

Once you set your goals and intentions, to get results faster, its best recommended that you forget about it entirely. What I mean is forget about what will be the outcome (good or bad). You should just focus on the journey of doing it with joy and happiness. Just enjoy every moment of your journey with those pure thoughts and massive action. Let go of your attachment on the outcome.

"Surrender yourself completely to higher powers."

5) Be in the state of Allowing

Let the universe decide when what should happen. If something terrible is happening to you accept it, allow it to happen, maybe the universe wants you to experience this so that you have some important lesson to learn from this experience. See the situation from the positive side and learn from the experience. If something good is happening, accept it, allow it to happen. Allow yourself to be in that flow of acceptance.

When you connect and trust the universe, you will evolve to your higher self, and you will have full abundance in all areas of your life.

*"**YOU** and only **YOU** have the **POWER** to change your life and live your life with PASSION, JOY, PEACE, LOVE, and HAPPINESS."*

MESSAGE FROM THE AUTHOR

Hope this book has given you tools required to move to your Higher Conscious levels and live your life with passion, joy, peace, love and happiness.

We (Souls) are here on this planet earth to have amazing life experiences. And to have these experiences, we need to move to higher conscious levels. And to move to your higher conscious levels, you have this 5-step model ready at hand.

This 5-step model has helped many people live their life with passion, joy, peace, love and happiness. I want you also to live your life with love, joy, peace, love and happiness because you are also a beautiful soul living on this planet earth and I want you also to have amazing life experiences.

Will you have amazing life experiences?

CONNECT WITH KUMAR

Kumar Nagendra –is India's leading Mind Power and Energy expert and a coach. Kumar is a professional speaker and an international certified trainer. He was trained by T Harv Eker and Blair Singer who are among top trainers and leaders of the world. Kumar is also certified trainer by Dr. Bharath Chandra, who is Asia's No 1 Success Coach.

Website: https://kumarnagendra.com

Get into my above website and connect with me for lifetime by subscribing my website to get regular updates about my latest blogs, videos, Seminars and workshops.

You can also connect with me at my below mail.

info@kumarnagendra.com

KUMAR NAGENDRA

PROGRAMS OFFERED BY KUMAR NAGENDRA:

1. Absolute Mind Champion - Unlock your Energies

This is a 2-day Intensive program, where you will learn how to become an Absolute Mind Champion and unlock your energies. This program will help you to Evolve to your higher self and increase your energy vibrations.

Below are some of the snaps from the 2-day program

2. Awaken Your Mind and Energies Seminar

This is a Seminar where you will uncover many findings about your own Mind power and Energies. This seminar Awakens you and helps you change your state of inertia and make you realize the importance your own energy and mind power.

For more information go to my website https://kumarnagendra.com

"JUST REMEMBER YOU ARE A WONDERFUL SOUL, HAVE AMAZING LIFE EXPERIENCES"
– Kumar Nagendra

Made in the USA
Monee, IL
07 July 2026

56550189R00111